Driving through life, while being mindful that
$h!+ happeneds

Restricted: "WTH" Journal

Purpose: For keepsake everyday memories.

Hello: *"I'm blank page, I was left here on purpose"*

Introduction

Parent awareness and guidance are seriously recommended.

Driving through life while being mindful that $h!+ happeneds journals offers a mix of **self-love, self-reflection, self-discovery, self-criticism, self-admiration, self-esteem, self-guidance, self-confidence, self-care, self-compassion, self-control, self-reliant, self-assessment, self-tolerance, self-consciousness, and self-worth** to embrace personal growth and deepen self-realization to live more intentionally in your purpose. The driving theme of the journal book is the notion that life is a journey, much like taking a drive. Each day presents a new opportunity to explore, learn, and evolve. Through guided prompts and exercises, the journal encourages individuals to contemplate their history, acknowledging the lessons learned and the growth achieved.

Driving through life, while being mindful that
$h!+ happeneds (Past, Present, and Ongoing)

Restricted: "Writing Tomorrow's History" Journal

For keepsake everyday memories.

FOR SAFETY & AWARENESSS
PLEASE, SLOW DOWN

In life, expect to encounter some speed bumps (real-life reflective and calming hindrances and challenges to maneuver over or around):
Adulting, bad decision, bad individuals, financial instability, them individuals, liars, hypocrites, sickness, errors, mistake, no empathy, relations hiccups, temptations, vises, attitudes, greed, hate, bad relationship, loss of jobs, maturity, separation, ideologies, failure, mother nature, profiling, politics, violations of rights, bigotry, unemployment, embarrassment, idiots, inequality, a "no" answer, deaths, separations, challenging days, scams, harassments, jealousy, pets, break-ups, family interactions, agendas, hospitalization, peacefulness, finance troubles, racism, theft against, loss of friendship, doubt, disagreements, ungratefulness, bullies, diagnosis, incarceration, dependency, addiction, abuse, raising or mentoring a 'know it all" child/youth, mental and physical fatigue, mental stress, exhaustion, pressure, laziness, co-workers, bias and prejudices, supervisors, unfavorable personnel and policies of an establishment, criminality or injustice, and etc.,

PLEASE PROCEED FORWARD

Going forward, you should expect to encounter some daily tip, viewpoint, or sentiment paralleling driving and living.

DON'T STOP!

Keep moving forward.

DAILY EXAMPLE
Check-in daily

☑ **Yes. ANOTHER ONE!** I am thankful for another day of life and another opportunity to do better and be better than my yesterdays and yesteryears. (Be grateful of each day to…)

Each day include a daily reminder or mantra of importance to love yourself:
"I Me"

Driving
> As it relates to driving.

through life
> As it relates to living.

while being mindful
> As it relates to being attentive and aware while driving and living your best life.

Mr. Old School

"Opinions won't change facts, but facts may change a few opinions or charge a few to reassess and question their facts."

-IMO

Driving through life, while being mindful that

0001 ANOTHER ONE! **DAILY Check-in EXAMPLE** *FT GHAMBE*

Woke-up __0546 Hrs__ on __11__ / NOV / _____   M T W T F (S) S   Hours of sleep __7__

Sunny__ Cloudy ✓ Rainy__ Stormy__ Lightning__ Windy__ WTHail__ Snow__ WTMother Nature__

Today, I AM

☐	☐	☑	☑	☐	☑	🛑 STOP	☐	☐	☐	☐	☐	☐
GREAT	HOPEFUL	(AWESOME)	(MINDFUL)	BOLD	(ENCOURAGED)		GROUCHY	HURT	ANGRY	MAD	BELLIGERENT	ENRAGED
GOOD	HAPPY	ACTIVE	(MOTIVATED)	BRILLIANT	ENERGIZED		GUARDED	HATEFUL	ANNOYED	MOODY	BITTER	EXHAUSTED

This $h!+ happeneds,

A place to write for self-awareness, clarity, tracking, self-confidence, growth, history, or about

an event, incident, interactions, location, visit, or encounter.

A place to write a daily positive, negative, all-most, aha, lesson learned, or never again.

A place for a service member to write a reminder, timeline, synopsis, or quick note to add to an

IR/SIR, DD FM 2910, Sworn Statement, SITREP, AAR, SPOTREP, Staff Journal, or Duty Log.

A place to write a specific record of Who, What, When, Where, Why, and How?

An unforgettable and tragic day.

A statement for or against.

A forever treasured day entry to share with future generations.

An action plan to a goal. To track and organize.

A journal entry of one's truth, illumination, or fact recently discovered (today years old).

Or A chance to add, disagree, vent, challenge, or feel likewise in print with each daily prompt.

_____

_____

_____

_____

Below last word section not to scale (space exaggerated to give example)

LAST WORD IN ("Best Moment of Today" – "My Final Thought on Today" – "NOPE!, Never Again"):

Another awesome day. **HAPPY VETERANS DAY!**

VETERANS, I ACKNOWLEDGE AND I APPRECIATE YOU.

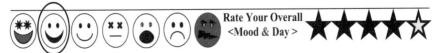

Rate Your Overall
<Mood & Day > ★ ★ ★ ★ ☆

$h!+ happeneds

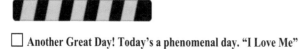

☐ **Another Great Day! Today's a phenomenal day. "I Love Me"**

Driving

Artificial Intelligence (AI) and autonomous technology is part of our automobile's future, but an autonomous vehicle must be programmed to function. Be aware that any autonomous technology connected to the cyber world can be hacked.

through life

An Awesome Individual (AI) is needed as part of a better future for humankind.

Be aware that your thinking, or interpretation could be hacked or has already been hacked.

1. Do you perform, search, and return information as a computer or as a companionate and thoughtful person?
2. Who built your Conscientious People Understanding (CPU) system?
3. Do you know if your system is corrupt, hacked, or requires an update?
4. Do you think and function independently or require software and data input?
5. Do you think you can be hacked or implanted with a dormant hateful and biased virus?
6. If hacked, when did you become aware of your hack?
7. How long have you been infected with that virus?
8. Who installed or had access to install a virus and corrupt your system?
9. Do installers know their system has been hacked?
10. Have you noticed any damage or conflict due to the hack?
11. Is your system slower than other systems?
12. Do you care if your system is hacked?
13. Are you easy to compromise, immune to being compromised, or require additional software protection from a virus or hacking?
14. If hacked. What's next? How do you keep yourself from being hacked again by another corrupted system (Individual, mentor, guru, leader, group, or media empire) attack?

while being mindful

It only takes one hacked racist, to infect others connected to their network. For you to thrive in a conducive and productive inclusive community or society, you must protect yourself from be corrupted and allow mindful and awareness updating to prevent new hateful platform (individuals or media mediums) viruses and you must continue to monitor all people routing into your kindness and humanism. You must act quickly against any known bigotry probes (jokes) or attempts and corruption.

Caution If you're infected by racism virus, you must:

1. Disconnect quickly and remove yourself from the network of corrupt individuals.
2. Change your way of thinking.
3. Identify the problem/source/vulnerability.
4. Scan for other possibilities of malicious bigotry intrusions.
5. Quarantine and remove hate.
6. Access damages to self and others connect to you.
7. Cleanse the hate and re-install kindness and humanism.
8. Remember to do some R&R (Recover & Reconnect).

Driving through life, while being mindful that

Woke-up _____ on ____/____/____   M T W T F S S   Hours of sleep ____

Sunny__ Cloudy__ Rainy__ Stormy__ Lightning__ Windy__ WTHail__ Snow__ WTMother Nature__

TODAY, I AM

☐	☐	☐	☐	☐	☐	🛑	☐	☐	☐	☐	☐	☐
GREAT	HOPEFUL	AWESOME	MINDFUL	BOLD	ENCOURAGED		GROUCHY	HURT	ANGRY	MAD	BELLIGERENT	ENRAGED
GOOD	HAPPY	ACTIVE	MOTIVATED	BRILLIANT	ENERGIZED		GUARDED	HATEFUL	ANNOYED	MOODY	BITTER	EXHAUSTED

TODAY, I AM GRATEFUL & EXCITED ABOUT:

_____

_____

_____

_____

_____

_____

_____

_____

_____

_____

_____

_____

_____

_____

_____

_____

_____

_____

_____

_____

_____

_____

_____

_____

LAST WORD IN ("Best Moment of Today" – "My Final Thought on Today" – "NOPE!, Never Again"):

$h!+ happeneds

☐ **Another Great Day! Today, where have you been all my life? "I Love Me"**

Driving

   If lost driving, you need to know when to stop and ask for assistance.

through life

   If you're alive, you have an opportunity. It's easy to lose your way, but don't.
   • Don't allow one mistake to uproot your life.
   • Don't allow addiction to take away your future.
   • Don't allow time in jail to stall your life.
   • Don't allow hate to desecrate and inflict more on your life than the hater.
   • Don't allow the bad in one relationship to squander the love that follows.

while being mindful

   Today, you are not where you want to be, but if you're driven, tomorrow can be the day reserved for you.

Today	Tomorrow
Lost	Found
Back up…	The Lead…
Assistant	Lead w/an assistant
Internship	Employee
Sub/Protégé	Teacher/Instructor
Dugout/"Riding Pine"/"Dressed out"	On the Field/In the game/On the Court
Pre-med	Doctor
Delay Entry	Service member
Divorced	Single or Re-married & Happiest
Fired/Lay off	New hirer/Entrepreneur
Runner Up/Loss	1st Place/Winner--Champion

Driving through life, while being mindful that

Woke-up _____ on _____/_____/_____   M T W T F S S   Hours of sleep ____

Sunny__ Cloudy__ Rainy__ Stormy__ Lightning__ Windy__ WTHail__ Snow__ WTMother Nature__

TODAY, I AM

□	□	□	□	□	□	STOP	□	□	□	□	□	□

GREAT   HOPEFUL   AWESOME   MINDFUL   BOLD   ENCOURAGED | GROUCHY   HURT   ANGRY   MAD   BELLIGERENT   ENRAGED

GOOD   HAPPY   ACTIVE   MOTIVATED BRILLIANT ENERGIZED | GUARDED   HATEFUL   ANNOYED   MOODY   BITTER   EXHAUSTED

TODAY, I AM GRATEFUL & EXCITED ABOUT:

_____

_____
_____
_____
_____
_____
_____
_____
_____
_____
_____
_____
_____
_____
_____
_____
_____
_____
_____
_____
_____
_____

LAST WORD IN ("Best Moment of Today" – "My Final Thought on Today" – "NOPE!, Never Again"):

$h!+ happeneds

☐ **Another Great Day! Yesterday, how do you like me now? "I Love Me"**

Driving

Every mechanic isn't a good mechanic. If two maintenance or repair shops give you conflicting analysis and cost, go to a third until you find an analysis and cost that is more comfortable for your finances and consciousness.

through life

Some people will try to take advantage of you and immediately assume their knowledge and experience outwit you.

while being mindful:

If the media use a salacious headline to draw you in, why wouldn't they use a salacious story to keep you? Remember--a media article, link, post, or breaking news report is one person's, blogger's, party, media group, or news agency's take on the truth, half-truth, or what they believe should be reported as the truth so help them, God.

Question yourself before re-posting

1. Is my social media re-posting to informed, inspired, or infuriated? **To answer this question**: Were you informed, inspired, or infuriated when you viewed or heard?

2. Is my social media re-post old, new, false, or truthful and is it being shared to divide, fund, or support an agenda?

3. Be careful and thoughtful in your words, response, action, or inactions. The foul individuals in your life will misconstrue what they believe you meant to say or do, not what you did or said.

Headspace and Timing Malfunctions Awareness (Hooah)

After assembling your response and before firing off with any words and actions toward anyone; always check yourself before you harm yourself or everyone in close danger (danger close). Whenever you invite someone into your conversation or actions; try to make sure they're as comfortable as you in that same space. Just know, some people won't be comfortable unless they're in their own physical space or headspace and they haven't cleared, changed, or fixed their headspace to be able to consider others.

Driving through life, while being mindful that

Woke-up _____ on ____/_____/_____   M T W T F S S   Hours of sleep ____

Sunny__ Cloudy__ Rainy__ Stormy__ Lightning__ Windy__ WTHail__ Snow__ WTMother Nature__

TODAY, I AM

☐	☐	☐	☐	☐	☐	STOP	☐	☐	☐	☐	☐	☐
GREAT	HOPEFUL	AWESOME	MINDFUL	BOLD	ENCOURAGED		GROUCHY	HURT	ANGRY	MAD	BELLIGERENT	ENRAGED
GOOD	HAPPY	ACTIVE	MOTIVATED	BRILLIANT	ENERGIZED		GUARDED	HATEFUL	ANNOYED	MOODY	BITTER	EXHAUSTED

TODAY, I AM GRATEFUL & EXCITED ABOUT:

_____

_____
_____
_____
_____
_____
_____
_____
_____
_____
_____
_____
_____
_____
_____
_____
_____
_____
_____
_____
_____
_____
_____
_____

LAST WORD IN ("Best Moment of Today" – "My Final Thought on Today" – "NOPE!, Never Again"):

$h!+ happeneds

☐ **Another Great Day! Peace on Earth & Peace Be Unto Me. "I Love Me"**

Driving

Even though the automotive commercials hope to have you believe one type of vehicle is supreme over all others, many are not.

through life

"**ONE RACE,** _____ _____ _____" not One Dominant Race or One Supreme Race.

It seems simple. One human race instead of one colossal inhumane, competing, power grabbing, and race status disgrace. Even though the rhetoric of some groups hopes to have you believe one race, gender, faith, or political party is supreme over all others, they aren't. You should never look across at another human as being lesser or more divine and deserving than you. Sadly, we're structured and indoctrinated to through media (news, televisions, movies, and sports) to believe everything is based on competition of two opposing sides (good/evil, foe/enemy, villain/hero, democratic/republican, my religion/your religions, my team/your team, my country/foreigners, poor/rich, rich/wealthy, my rights/rights, and white/non-whites) but we're all the same more than different. We're so appreciative of anything being at 100% authentic and genuine but continue to settle on 50-50 for humanity. Our tax dollars fund our leaders and government representatives to continue divide US near and far. Wars continue to generate wealth for everyone except the citizens (same companies/same big contractors). Our leader will insist that jobs will be created in the rebuild as the result of war's destruction but never comment on the rebuilding of the lives obliterated by wars unless putting forward a bill for more program by tax dollars (w/o distribution transparency).

Past Post-War Mentality: Countries and their economies were built after conflicts and wars over boundaries ("Our piece of land pie").

Present: No country builds up a war arsenal for training only or for equipment to sit in depots. The threat of wars sustains countries, boundaries, and their economies (military equipment trade).

On-Going: The threat of wars will continue to sustain countries and their economies.

while being mindful

- Great leaders become great when they right the wrong of past leaders.
- All leaders are not destined to lead; some happen by default, luck, error, facade, scam, agendas, privilege, wealth, the process of elimination, or death.
- Some individuals, influencers, orators, and speakers gained their gift of gab to persuade, manipulate, and coerce after years of errors and criminality by memorizing, experimenting, learning, practicing, disguising, collaborating, and perfecting the best way to fake, scam, deceive, and steal.

Perfect People? Nobody's life is perfect, but many are capable of perfecting how others visualize, capture, or report their life.

Woke-up _____ on ____/_____/_____   M T W T F S S   Hours of sleep ____

Sunny__ Cloudy__ Rainy__ Stormy__ Lightning__ Windy__ WTHail__ Snow__ WTMother Nature__

TODAY, I AM

☐   ☐   ☐   ☐   ☐   ☐   **STOP**   ☐   ☐   ☐   ☐   ☐   ☐

GREAT   HOPEFUL   AWESOME   MINDFUL   BOLD   ENCOURAGED   GROUCHY   HURT   ANGRY   MAD   BELLIGERENT   ENRAGED

GOOD   HAPPY   ACTIVE   MOTIVATED   BRILLIANT   ENERGIZED   GUARDED   HATEFUL   ANNOYED   MOODY   BITTER   EXHAUSTED

TODAY, I AM GRATEFUL & EXCITED ABOUT:

_____

_____

_____

_____

_____

_____

_____

_____

_____

_____

_____

_____

_____

_____

_____

_____

_____

_____

_____

_____

_____

_____

_____

_____

_____

LAST WORD IN ("Best Moment of Today" – "My Final Thought on Today" – "NOPE!, Never Again"):

$h!+ happeneds

☐ **Another Great Day! I have another day to be more and do more. "I Love Me"**

Driving

Operating a vehicle is not as complex as owning or being solely responsible for the vehicle's taxes, insurance, gas, damages, and maintenance costs.

through life

The physical part of a relationship isn't as complex as being responsible for what occurs afterward to both or at least one's mind, spirit, feeling, body, responsibilities, or reality.

while being mindful

Try mind before heart and heart before flesh because doing it in reverse usually ends in a mess.

Woke-up _____ on ____/____/_____   M T W T F S S   Hours of sleep ____

Sunny_ Cloudy_ Rainy_ Stormy_ Lightning_ Windy_ WTHail_ Snow_ WTMother Nature__

TODAY, I AM

☐ GREAT   ☐ HOPEFUL   ☐ AWESOME   ☐ MINDFUL   ☐ BOLD   ☐ ENCOURAGED   **STOP**   ☐ GROUCHY   ☐ HURT   ☐ ANGRY   ☐ MAD   ☐ BELLIGERENT   ☐ ENRAGED

GOOD   HAPPY   ACTIVE   MOTIVATED   BRILLIANT   ENERGIZED   GUARDED   HATEFUL   ANNOYED   MOODY   BITTER   EXHAUSTED

TODAY, I AM GRATEFUL & EXCITED ABOUT:

_____

_____

_____

_____

_____

_____

_____

_____

_____

_____

_____

_____

_____

_____

_____

_____

_____

_____

_____

_____

_____

_____

_____

_____

_____

_____

LAST WORD IN ("Best Moment of Today" – "My Final Thought on Today" – "NOPE!, Never Again"):

$h!+ happeneds

☐ **Another Great Day! It begins with me. I will be awesome today. "I Love Me"**

Driving
> Boot vs. Towed vs. Repo (all costly)

through life
> Hospitalization vs. Jail vs. Prison (each comes with a cost)

while being mindful
> 3-5minutes-better life vs. 3-5 people to talk or listen vs. 3-5yrs-life
> Calming yourself with 3 to 5 minutes of your favorite songs is better than doing 3 to 5 years. Venting your anger or displeasure to 3 to 5 friends or family members is better than doing 3 to 5 years because you didn't de-escalate your anger.

<u>**Reminder**</u>
Most bedrooms, even some bathrooms, are bigger and have more amenities and privacy than a jail or prison cell; so, why would anyone choose a lifestyle (criminal act) that almost guarantees them up to 22 hours a day in WAAAYYY too small of a square foot environment? Will your buddy you're doing dirt with be enthused as your enthused about the same accommodations? Will your girl you're doing dirt with be enthused as you're enthused about the same accommodations? Will the individual you're having a physical altercation with be as enthused as you're enthused about the accommodation?

<u>**Additional ways to do 3-5 minutes to a better life before changing a life or lives drastically or forever.**</u>
Watch a 3–5 minutes video
Go outside for 3–5 minutes for some fresh air.
Make a 3–5 minutes phone call to family or friend.
Read a literary favorite that lasts at least 3–5 minutes.
Converse with 3-5 new possibilities for 3–5 minutes to hopefully celebrate one of your best anniversaries in 3-55.

Woke-up _____ on ____/____/_____   M T W T F S S   Hours of sleep ____

Sunny__ Cloudy__ Rainy__ Stormy__ Lightning__ Windy__ WTHail__ Snow__ WTMother Nature__

TODAY, I AM

☐	☐	☐	☐	☐	☐	STOP	☐	☐	☐	☐	☐	☐
GREAT	HOPEFUL	AWESOME	MINDFUL	BOLD	ENCOURAGED		GROUCHY	HURT	ANGRY	MAD	BELLIGERENT	ENRAGED
GOOD	HAPPY	ACTIVE	MOTIVATED	BRILLIANT	ENERGIZED		GUARDED	HATEFUL	ANNOYED	MOODY	BITTER	EXHAUSTED

TODAY, I AM GRATEFUL & EXCITED ABOUT:

_____

_____

_____

_____

_____

_____

_____

_____

_____

_____

_____

_____

_____

_____

_____

_____

_____

_____

_____

_____

_____

_____

_____

_____

_____

LAST WORD IN ("Best Moment of Today" – "My Final Thought on Today" – "NOPE!, Never Again"):

$h!+ happeneds

☐ **Another Great Day! Let's do this. "I Love Me"**

Driving

You will gain more confidence by driving. Every time you drive and return home safely builds confidence in driving. Driving many diverse types of vehicles doesn't make you a better driver. You become a better driver by driving.

through life

You gain more confidence by practicing, training, and experiencing life.

You get better at being a better person, friend, or companion through repetition.

You become a professional by wanting to be professional at something specific.

You become an expert by wanting more knowledge than others.

You become a college graduate by wanting to attend college than not.

You become a highly recommended tradesman by wanting to attend the nontraditional route.

You become a proud military veteran by wanting to serve.

while being mindful.

Doing builds confidence, so before you "practice what you preach," practice preaching.

In life, you inevitably become better by doing, but will it be:

1. Good or bad?
2. Legal or illegal?
3. Self-inflicted/pace or peer pressured?
4. Excused by or blamed for naïve or unknowingly?
5. Immoral or morally, right?
6. Blaming or taking blame?
7. Faulted due to being passive or assertive?
8. For the constituents or for you?
9. For the constituents or for the party?
10. For the laws, constitution, and citizen's rights or for your ideologies?

What should a new driver expect to hear?

"You Scared? Don't mess up! Do you know what you are doing? Too fast! Stop Sweating, Gas/Brake! Wait! Seat belt. Put the car in drive/park/reverse. Use mirrors. Hurry up! Are you Ready? I can't. Slow Down, Lookout! Stop! Are you sure? Could you give it a little gas? Relax. Move over, Too fast. Too Slow. That was close. Too close. Too much. Stop grinding the gears. Too wide. Stay in your lane. Look over your shoulder. Just drive. I'm not too fond of parallel parking. Stay focused on your driving. You got this. No distractions. You made it home safely.

*<u>One positivity for new drivers</u>: As you drive more, you will stop saying everything above to yourself.

Woke-up _____ on _____/_____/_____   M T W T F S S   Hours of sleep ____

Sunny__ Cloudy__ Rainy__ Stormy__ Lightning__ Windy__ WTHail__ Snow__ WTMother Nature__

TODAY, I AM

☐ ☐ ☐ ☐ ☐ ☐ **STOP** ☐ ☐ ☐ ☐ ☐ ☐

| GREAT | HOPEFUL | AWESOME | MINDFUL | BOLD | ENCOURAGED | | GROUCHY | HURT | ANGRY | MAD | BELLIGERENT | ENRAGED |
| GOOD | HAPPY | ACTIVE | MOTIVATED | BRILLIANT | ENERGIZED | | GUARDED | HATEFUL | ANNOYED | MOODY | BITTER | EXHAUSTED |

TODAY, I AM GRATEFUL & EXCITED ABOUT:

_____

_____

_____

_____

_____

_____

_____

_____

_____

_____

_____

_____

_____

_____

_____

_____

_____

_____

_____

_____

_____

_____

_____

_____

_____

LAST WORD IN ("Best Moment of Today" – "My Final Thought on Today" – "NOPE!, Never Again"):

$h!+ happeneds

☐ **Another Great Day! Under the influence of life. "I Love Me"**

Driving

Drinking and Driving is against the law? Driving Under the Influence (DUI) is the crime or offense of driving or operating a motor vehicle while impaired by alcohol or other drugs.

through life

Living Under the Influence (LUI) is the negative spirit of living or interacting with others while impaired, misled, controlled, brainwashed, or misinformed by a person, group, society, media, cult, or organization's falsehoods. Influenced to a level that renders the person incapable of making a safe, sound, or rationalized decision on their own.

while being mindful:

Additionally, don't live your adult life under the influence of these "I's":

1. Individualism
2. Idiocy
3. Ignorance
4. Irresponsibility
5. Idiotism
6. Impoverished
7. Injurious
8. Infuriated
9. Injustice
10. Ideology
11. Inhospitable
12. Intoxication
13. Insanity
14. Impossible
15. Imbecile
16. Insubordinate
17. Inhumane
18. Ignoramus
19. Imposter
20. Insecure
21. Immaturity
22. Incarceration
23. Institutionalization

Woke-up _____ on ____/____/____ M T W T F S S   Hours of sleep ____

Sunny__ Cloudy__ Rainy__ Stormy__ Lightning__ Windy__ WTHail__ Snow__ WTMother Nature__

TODAY, I AM

☐	☐	☐	☐	☐	☐	STOP	☐	☐	☐	☐	☐	☐
GREAT	HOPEFUL	AWESOME	MINDFUL	BOLD	ENCOURAGED		GROUCHY	HURT	ANGRY	MAD	BELLIGERENT	ENRAGED
GOOD	HAPPY	ACTIVE	MOTIVATED	BRILLIANT	ENERGIZED		GUARDED	HATEFUL	ANNOYED	MOODY	BITTER	EXHAUSTED

TODAY, I AM GRATEFUL & EXCITED ABOUT:

_____

_____

_____

_____

_____

_____

_____

_____

_____

_____

_____

_____

_____

_____

_____

_____

_____

_____

_____

_____

_____

_____

_____

_____

LAST WORD IN ("Best Moment of Today" – "My Final Thought on Today" – "NOPE!, Never Again"):

$h!+ happeneds

☐ **Another Great Day! Be happy today. Smile today.** 😊 **"I Love Me"**_____

Driving

> I was planning to have the car's engine repaired, but now the engine is kaput and requires replacing.

through life

> I was planning to do better but it was too late.
> I was planning to change, but now it's over.

while being mindful

> Yes, there's "Me time" before "We time," but it can revert quickly to "Me time" if "Me" time doesn't plug back into "We" time.
> **Choices**: Spouse, kids, family, close friends, or Self.

> <u>Choose wisely</u>

> I choose We time over Me time.
> I choose Us time.
> I choose We
> Or

> Sometimes I choose We
> Sometimes I choose Me
> Sometimes?
> Or

> I choose Me time over We time.
> I choose Me time.
> I choose Me.

Some people? You know Da Kine.
Some people know better but choose the opposite.
Some people need to be guided and shown better to know better.
Some people don't give a hoot about being better or the betterment of others.
Choose the people who know better, do better, and treat you better.

Driving through life, while being mindful that

Woke-up _____ on ____/____/_____   M T W T F S S   Hours of sleep ____

Sunny__ Cloudy__ Rainy__ Stormy__ Lightning__ Windy__ WTHail__ Snow__ WTMother Nature__

TODAY, I AM

☐	☐	☐	☐	☐	☐	STOP	☐	☐	☐	☐	☐	☐
GREAT	HOPEFUL	AWESOME	MINDFUL	BOLD	ENCOURAGED		GROUCHY	HURT	ANGRY	MAD	BELLIGERENT	ENRAGED
GOOD	HAPPY	ACTIVE	MOTIVATED	BRILLIANT	ENERGIZED		GUARDED	HATEFUL	ANNOYED	MOODY	BITTER	EXHAUSTED

TODAY, I AM GRATEFUL & EXCITED ABOUT:

_____

_____

_____

_____

_____

_____

_____

_____

_____

_____

_____

_____

_____

_____

_____

_____

_____

_____

_____

_____

_____

_____

_____

LAST WORD IN ("Best Moment of Today" – "My Final Thought on Today" – "NOPE!, Never Again"):

$h!+ happeneds

☐ **Another Great Day! Fo Schism. "I Love Me"**

Some Ism schismnism

- If racism, colorism, and anti-racism encompasses many races; why doesn't each labeled race have their own specific labeled ism? Is ownership required? **What do dark skin tone people own** officially, federally, or globally to specifically cry anti-outrage over it when its violated, trampled against, or has hostile behavior toward? ~~A Religion, African American identity, light or dark-skinned title, Culture, "N" word, Slavery, African Lineage, Ancestral Traditions, Wealth, Critical Race Theory, Slang, Southern Food Cuisine, Music Industry, Music Genre (R&B/HipHop)~~, or ~~Wall Street~~. NONE

- What black celebration day do Americans, Irish, or Irish Americans go out to spend $$$ as they celebrate as St. Patrick Day? What MLK Day restaurant is the meeting spot? What black celebration do Americans, Mexicans, or Mexican Americans go out to spend and celebrate at a black establishment as Cinco De Mayo? JUNETEENTH?

- If our government and current elected officials are still allowing human beings to be specifically separated, labeled, singled out by a race identity; shouldn't anyone of those races be allowed or request the media be specific about their own ism instead of racism? What type of racism? Blackism, anti-Blackism, African Americanism, anti-Africanism, Asianism, Latin Americanism, or Racist against _____. Racism against whom? If a stated race of racism wasn't given for an individual's racism; would you know who's was being discriminated or whom there is an outcry of, toward, or against.

- Ism I right or Ism I wrong, or
  Ism I just needing to be quiet, dribble, or a little more patient for the words involving or associated with "race identity" to be stricken or updated officially one ~~day~~ decade ahead?

Ism I right or Ism I wrong

- Ism I right or Ism I wrong- To be viewed as a successful United States President, you only need to show your constituents that you attempted to complete 25-35% of what you campaigned. It is like investing in a new-trending bitcoin with an unknown guru without any known financial background or history and expecting a major return in your investment. A guru whose history is available if researched but of no concern until the guru flees the country, files for bankruptcy, or faces a federal indictment.

- Ism I right or Ism I wrong- To be viewed as being loyal to your political party over constituents as a senator or congressman, you must vote with the majority or with the president of the party.

- Ism I right or Ism I wrong- Our political representatives are outrage at individuals seeking asylum at borders but distance and silence for the same individuals working illegally on farmlands, construction, or lower than fair market value laborer jobs. Individuals hired to work until discoveries and an investigation forces the employers to release the same statement of "No Knowledge" and pay fine. Make billions to afford penalties of millions or continue contract while blaming and faulting sub-contractors.

- Ism I right or Ism I wrong- Why do our leaders represent they're not in favor how a foreign group uses their religion to dictate and strip away the rights of citizens but be drooling and "damn near" doing the same under the umbrella of conservatism ism ism?

Driving through life, while being mindful that

Woke-up _____ on ____/____/_____   M T W T F S S   Hours of sleep ____

Sunny__ Cloudy__ Rainy__ Stormy__ Lightning__ Windy__ WTHail__ Snow__ WTMother Nature__

TODAY, I AM

☐	☐	☐	☐	☐	☐	**STOP**	☐	☐	☐	☐	☐	☐
GREAT	HOPEFUL	AWESOME	MINDFUL	BOLD	ENCOURAGED		GROUCHY	HURT	ANGRY	MAD	BELLIGERENT	ENRAGED
GOOD	HAPPY	ACTIVE	MOTIVATED	BRILLIANT	ENERGIZED		GUARDED	HATEFUL	ANNOYED	MOODY	BITTER	EXHAUSTED

TODAY, I AM GRATEFUL & EXCITED ABOUT:

_____

_____

_____

_____

_____

_____

_____

_____

_____

_____

_____

_____

_____

_____

_____

_____

_____

_____

_____

_____

_____

_____

LAST WORD IN ("Best Moment of Today" – "My Final Thought on Today" – "NOPE!, Never Again"):

_____

_____

$h!+ happeneds

☐ **Another Great Day! The journey continues. "I Love Me"**

Driving

Don't be so quick to maneuver over and behind the next vehicle coming from your rear because a low unloaded trailer could be attached to their vehicle.

through life

Don't be so quick to follow (bandwagon) the next wonderful thing by a slick talker, con, influencer, or leader without pause, research, observation, evaluation, and confirmation.

while being mindful

Back the fudge up and think about how much you're putting into something before it becomes too difficult to change or stop.

Are all fruits excellent or bad?

If you believe every online search returned, fruits could be good or bad and healthy or unhealthy depending on the most persuasive result or advertisement funded top search result. Depending on your search, an apple is Loved (daily), Hated (acidic, sugar), Recommended (nutritious), Only in moderation (carbs), Natural only (pesticide?), or Recommend fresh and raw only (fiber).

The moral of any fruit story: Polls, statistics, reviews, and recommendations sound bites are great until you find out who wrote, maneuvered, manipulate, lobbied, or funded the study, numbers, social media placement, or paid for the individual(s) media post or recommendation.

Woke-up _____ on _____/_____/_____ M T W T F S S   Hours of sleep _____

Sunny__ Cloudy__ Rainy__ Stormy__ Lightning__ Windy__ WTHail__ Snow__ WTMother Nature__

TODAY, I AM

☐ ☐ ☐ ☐ ☐ ☐ `STOP` ☐ ☐ ☐ ☐ ☐ ☐

GREAT	HOPEFUL	AWESOME	MINDFUL	BOLD	ENCOURAGED		GROUCHY	HURT	ANGRY	MAD	BELLIGERENT	ENRAGED
GOOD	HAPPY	ACTIVE	MOTIVATED	BRILLIANT	ENERGIZED		GUARDED	HATEFUL	ANNOYED	MOODY	BITTER	EXHAUSTED

TODAY, I AM GRATEFUL & EXCITED ABOUT:

_____

_____
_____
_____
_____
_____
_____
_____
_____
_____
_____
_____
_____
_____
_____
_____
_____
_____
_____
_____
_____
_____
_____
_____

LAST WORD IN ("Best Moment of Today" – "My Final Thought on Today" – "NOPE!, Never Again"):

$h!+ happeneds

☐ **Another Great Day! IHAAATE People!** (*see as defined*) **"I Love Me"**

Driving

>Don't ride around with passengers that don't deserve and appreciate your driving.

through life

>Don't associate or befriend individuals who don't deserve and appreciate you.

while being mindful

>Racism is like a virus because it needs immediate attention and must be quarantined and eradicated quickly, or it will spread. Be cautious of "Self-imposed Truer Americans" A selected few who tell others to go back from where they came and overtly display, wave, and flaunt their Americanism in front of fellow Americans (military included) like it makes them a better or prouder American. "The few, the too out loud" **EXAMPLES**: We WHAAATE Americans should not discuss in today's school any specific history of AMERICANS categorizes and labeled sub-AMERICAN by our past European-Americans, especially in regards to America's unfavorable and genocide history of those fellow AMERICANS. We WHAAATE Americans are against any favorable history of AMERICANS identified as Half-AMERICANS or a race within AMERICA. We WHAAATE Americans are against our American children having any knowledge of AMERICANS we WHAAATE Americans consider not Full-AMERICAN. We WHAAATE Americans are offended by the history (positive or negative) of any AMERICAN that we WHAAATE Americans consider lesser than WHAAATE American. We WHAAATE Americans must continue to change to laws to keep AMERICA in the hands of Truer WHAAATE Americans not SUB-AMERICANS such as AFRICAN AMERICAN, ASIAN AMERICAN, AMERICAN INDIAN, PACIFIC ISLAND AMERICAN, AMERICAN SOMOAN, NATIVE AMERICAN, HISPANIC AMERICAN, or LATIN AMERICAN, and especially the unpredictable and uncontrollable voters of YOUNG AMERICANS.

Did you know that a governor's Dehumanization Encourages Segregationist Anarchistic Nonsense To Incite Supporters and their Disinformation Enables Supremacist Authoritarianism Nonsense To Invade Society. Dehumanization and disinformation that
Fails, Undermines, Controls, and Kills the United States internally and harm our allies' relations.

Woke-up _____ on ____/____/____   M T W T F S S   Hours of sleep ____

Sunny__ Cloudy__ Rainy__ Stormy__ Lightning__ Windy__ WTHail__ Snow__ WTMother Nature__

TODAY, I AM

GREAT	HOPEFUL	AWESOME	MINDFUL	BOLD	ENCOURAGED	STOP	GROUCHY	HURT	ANGRY	MAD	BELLIGERENT	ENRAGED
GOOD	HAPPY	ACTIVE	MOTIVATED	BRILLIANT	ENERGIZED		GUARDED	HATEFUL	ANNOYED	MOODY	BITTER	EXHAUSTED

TODAY, I AM GRATEFUL & EXCITED ABOUT:

_____

_____

_____

_____

_____

_____

_____

_____

_____

_____

_____

_____

_____

_____

_____

_____

_____

_____

_____

_____

_____

_____

_____

LAST WORD IN ("Best Moment of Today" – "My Final Thought on Today" – "NOPE!, Never Again"):

$h!+ happeneds

☐ **Another Great Day! WHAAATE a minute. I am resilient. "I Love Me"**

Be careful of the Hate Group's lie:
For you to be considered an allied member of any self-described distinguished and honorable hate group organization; you must share these applied beliefs:

1. It would be best if you believed in alienating yourself from all who think and speak freely and open-mindedly about you.
2. It would be best to ignore and not allow yourself to be bullied into believing any information outside the group informed and championed lies, even when your own eyes, ears, and intellect believes other evidential facts and truths supplied. You must believe protests, marches, and assemblies are to unite only and not used to program hate or advocate some to practice hatred and violence toward others.
3. You must believe the outside appearance of an individual to tell you everything about that person. In lieu of meeting, knowing, or discovering our foretold lies as lies; believe US.
4. You must believe anyone who doesn't agree or join in our beliefs is lost instead of you being the lost one. You must believe illegal aliens will future voters of non-believers.
5. You must believe your outside appearance automatically makes you intelligent, superior, and chosen, not your mind, body, spirit, or ancestral privilege.
6. If you're pained by life, it's only relieved by or through another race being pained.
7. You must believe your religious enlightening is relied on or only bestowed upon you by or through another human's leadership, anointment, blessings or prophetfiting; not you
8. You must believe you're not being lied to or misled to believe money is not essential to the leader you're following or isn't the root purpose of why the group was established.
9. You must believe we have the right to free speech and everyone else is to be bullied into believing it or have their freedom to speech rights taken away, be arrested, or deported.
10. Per our political clientele, you must continue to have disbelief in our voting system. As our past racist brothers and sisters lied and bullied to gain, we continue the same to sustain.
11. Lastly, you must be resilient with all the above beliefs and acknowledge that all words and contradictions against our current hate co-inspirer's, media liar's and in-the-pocket political conniver's beliefs are LIEs.

No harm, No Foul. A lie is someone's truth
1. Is there such a thing as a Good Lie, Small Tale Lie, or Fib?
    a. Would you or Do you lie for confidence building and encouragement?
    b. Would you or Do you lie for story and tall tales' embellishments (Tooth Fairy/Santa)?
    c. Would you or Do you lie because the truth hurt?
    d. Would you or Do you lie because it's a norm or it's done to you?
    e. Would you or Do you lie to protect yourself or someone else?
    f. Are you a liar? ____ By its definition, have you lied? ____ Will you lie again? No / Liar
2. Truth: A definitive decision for your life should be based on truth, not lies, and never both. There are no such things as a small lie because it always grows as more lies are stacked on top of it and those stacks do inevitably topple over and disrupt or change the individuals involved.

Driving through life, while being mindful that

Woke-up _____ on ____/____/____   M T W T F S S   Hours of sleep ____

Sunny__ Cloudy__ Rainy__ Stormy__ Lightning__ Windy__ WTHail__ Snow__ WTMother Nature__

TODAY, I AM

☐	☐	☐	☐	☐	☐		☐	☐	☐	☐	☐	☐
GREAT	HOPEFUL	AWESOME	MINDFUL	BOLD	ENCOURAGED	STOP	GROUCHY	HURT	ANGRY	MAD	BELLIGERENT	ENRAGED
GOOD	HAPPY	ACTIVE	MOTIVATED	BRILLIANT	ENERGIZED		GUARDED	HATEFUL	ANNOYED	MOODY	BITTER	EXHAUSTED

TODAY, I AM GRATEFUL & EXCITED ABOUT:

_____

_____

_____

_____

_____

_____

_____

_____

_____

_____

_____

_____

_____

_____

_____

_____

_____

_____

_____

_____

_____

_____

LAST WORD IN ("Best Moment of Today" – "My Final Thought on Today" – "NOPE!, Never Again"):

$h!+ happeneds

☐ **Another Great Day! Spectacular. "I Love Me"**

Driving

You don't automatically become a better or safer driver as you age.

It's good to be confident in your driving ability, but you're not the only one on the road, and overconfidence in your driving can lead to reckless driving or an accident. Don't partake in illegal road racing and expect to drive away when your involvement results in an injury or death.

through life

You don't automatically become a better person as you age, and you don't escape the consequences of your actions by changing.

while being mindful

Never think your ego is the only ego present in any room. Overconfidence can lead to awkwardness and mistakes.

- It only takes one momentary lapse of judgment.
- It only takes one momentarily lapse of judgment to lose a $20hr job for $20 or less worth of drugs or stolen property.
- It only takes one momentarily lapse of judgment to lose 20yrs of relations or marriage for less than 20 minutes or 20 seconds of ecstasy.
- It only takes one momentarily lapse of judgment to lose 20yrs of friendship for less than 20 seconds of gossiping or posting about something entrusted to you.
- It only takes one momentarily lapse of judgement to lose 5-10yrs of your freedom for less than 5-10 minutes of reported 'loss of insanity' or purported hustling, slanging, or banging.

The past (a year ago, an hour ago, or a few seconds ago)

Don't partake in illegal activity and expect to walk away without suffering because of your past involvement, self-righteousness, silence, selfishness, or blind eyes.

FT GHAMBE

Woke-up _____ on ____/____/_____ M T W T F S S   Hours of sleep ____

Sunny__ Cloudy__ Rainy__ Stormy__ Lightning__ Windy__ WTHail__ Snow__ WTMother Nature__

TODAY, I AM

☐	☐	☐	☐	☐	☐	STOP	☐	☐	☐	☐	☐	☐
GREAT	HOPEFUL	AWESOME	MINDFUL	BOLD	ENCOURAGED		GROUCHY	HURT	ANGRY	MAD	BELLIGERENT	ENRAGED
GOOD	HAPPY	ACTIVE	MOTIVATED	BRILLIANT	ENERGIZED		GUARDED	HATEFUL	ANNOYED	MOODY	BITTER	EXHAUSTED

TODAY, I AM GRATEFUL & EXCITED ABOUT:

_____

_____

_____

_____

_____

_____

_____

_____

_____

_____

_____

_____

_____

_____

_____

_____

_____

_____

_____

_____

_____

_____

_____

_____

_____

LAST WORD IN ("Best Moment of Today" – "My Final Thought on Today" – "NOPE!, Never Again"):

$h!+ happeneds

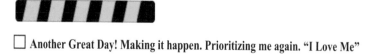

☐ **Another Great Day! Making it happen. Prioritizing me again. "I Love Me"**

Driving

There are always other drivers dependent and hopeful you do your part in the safe operation of your vehicle.

through life

Do your part each day. We all have a gift. Some have a gift to shape and guide a few individuals, while others can shape many. We all have a part in shaping the future. The personal and professional interaction you have with someone today will shape their next interaction.

while being mindful

Do your part. Everyone has the power to produce pure, influential positive people energy.

1. One person's act of kindness can shape several into doing a kind act.
2. One outstanding military leader can shape several into great senior military leaders.
3. One passionate teacher can shape several students to be passionate about learning and teaching in their future.
4. One person speaking against racism can shape several to speak up against it.
5. One news agency not focusing on the opposite or political divide can shape several local news to deliver the same consciously. Viewership can change any media's focus.
6. Your one local, state, and federal vote power can shape into the power to change our dated political leaders or system to change:
   - Numerous terms allowed. Two-party monopoly and governing institutes. 50/50
   - SCOTUS lifetime appointments.
   - Politicians being legally protected/shielded while in office.
   - Stop allowing politicians to misconstrue constituents as constickittothems.
   - Limit and control campaign salacious false ads, donations, and Political Action Committees (PAC-man) money ~~laundering~~ movement.

Does money taint our democratic system (pay to sustain)?

1. Which candidate has raised the most money through a special PAC (billionaires) buying ads?
2. Which candidate will assist their donor's bottom line when elected with bills, contracts, tax incentives, or uncontrolled lobbying influencing?
3. Who's making the most of their political dollars off citizens' back and forth bickering? Hint: Print & Media ads dollars going to or toward who…

What is PISS-POOR POLITICS (PPP)?

Is it Patriotism, Insurrection, Seditious, Suppression of votes tactics rearing its ugly head?
Claims of a rigged democratic election has caused citizens uproar and politicians to rig elections going forward. Voting changes that's only seems needed when the empowered lose power/votes.
PPP: Let us use our old favorite; gerrymandering is still a go. We will continue to allow a few wayward colleagues to rant of rigged elections to donors, fuel party divide, unless we win.
PPP: We must push to change laws to remove a representative or votes in case of loss and we must distract & hinder the unpredictable young voters. **Voting Assistance** www.fvap.gov

Driving through life, while being mindful that

FT GHAMBE

Woke-up _____ on _____/_____/_____   M T W T F S S   Hours of sleep ____

Sunny__ Cloudy__ Rainy__ Stormy__ Lightning__ Windy__ WTHail__ Snow__ WTMother Nature__

TODAY, I AM

☐	☐	☐	☐	☐	☐	STOP	☐	☐	☐	☐	☐	☐
GREAT	HOPEFUL	AWESOME	MINDFUL	BOLD	ENCOURAGED		GROUCHY	HURT	ANGRY	MAD	BELLIGERENT	ENRAGED
GOOD	HAPPY	ACTIVE	MOTIVATED	BRILLIANT	ENERGIZED		GUARDED	HATEFUL	ANNOYED	MOODY	BITTER	EXHAUSTED

TODAY, I AM GRATEFUL & EXCITED ABOUT:

_____

_____

_____

_____

_____

_____

_____

_____

_____

_____

_____

_____

_____

_____

_____

_____

_____

_____

_____

_____

_____

_____

_____

_____

_____

LAST WORD IN ("Best Moment of Today" – "My Final Thought on Today" – "NOPE!, Never Again"):

$h!+ happeneds

☐ **Another Great Day! A momentous day to be me. "I Love Me"**

Driving

Never mess with someone's vehicle without their permission. Don't touch their vehicle without their permission. Don't open or force entry into their vehicle (door, hood, or trunk). Don't put your face close to look inside their vehicle (leave your palm & breath). Going underneath a vehicle of another is wrong (converters). Even if you have ridden inside their vehicle, it doesn't authorize you anything regarding their vehicle.

through life

- To Violate: fail to respect (someone's space, peace, privacy, or rights).
- To Assault: make a physical attack on. a violent physical or verbal attack.
- To Harass: to annoy or bother(someone) in a constant or repeated way.

while being mindful

Every person's definition of violating, assaulting, and harassing differs but you will have a tough time convincing a jury of your peers to agree that your definition outweighs the complainant or victim.

Woke-up _____ on ____/____/____   M T W T F S S   Hours of sleep ____

Sunny__ Cloudy__ Rainy__ Stormy__ Lightning__ Windy__ WTHail__ Snow__ WTMother Nature__

TODAY, I AM

☐	☐	☐	☐	☐	☐	STOP	☐	☐	☐	☐	☐	☐
GREAT	HOPEFUL	AWESOME	MINDFUL	BOLD	ENCOURAGED		GROUCHY	HURT	ANGRY	MAD	BELLIGERENT	ENRAGED
GOOD	HAPPY	ACTIVE	MOTIVATED	BRILLIANT	ENERGIZED		GUARDED	HATEFUL	ANNOYED	MOODY	BITTER	EXHAUSTED

TODAY, I AM GRATEFUL & EXCITED ABOUT:

_____

_____

_____

_____

_____

_____

_____

_____

_____

_____

_____

_____

_____

_____

_____

_____

_____

_____

_____

_____

_____

_____

_____

LAST WORD IN ("Best Moment of Today" – "My Final Thought on Today" – "NOPE!, Never Again"):

$h!+ happeneds

☐ **Another Great Day! I'm something special. "I Love Me"**

Driving

Some days, you will be stuck in traffic, and some days, you will travel in the opposite direction of congested traffic.

through life

Be thankful for the days you're viewing a mess instead of being the cause or part of the mess.

while being mindful

Just because someone makes their lifestyle sound better; doesn't make it better than yours.

Half-full or Half-empty?

- Are 365 days of incarceration in a county jail for selling illegal drugs better than 12 months in jail?
- Are 8,760 hours remaining on probation for a snatch-and-grab robbery better than starting one year of probation?
- Is 36 months sleeping on a bunk in prison better than three years.

Woke-up _____ on ____/____/____ M T W T F S S Hours of sleep ____

Sunny__ Cloudy__ Rainy__ Stormy__ Lightning__ Windy__ WTHail__ Snow__ WTMother Nature__

TODAY, I AM

☐	☐	☐	☐	☐	☐	STOP	☐	☐	☐	☐	☐	☐
GREAT	HOPEFUL	AWESOME	MINDFUL	BOLD	ENCOURAGED		GROUCHY	HURT	ANGRY	MAD	BELLIGERENT	ENRAGED
GOOD	HAPPY	ACTIVE	MOTIVATED	BRILLIANT	ENERGIZED		GUARDED	HATEFUL	ANNOYED	MOODY	BITTER	EXHAUSTED

TODAY, I AM GRATEFUL & EXCITED ABOUT:

_____

_____
_____
_____
_____
_____
_____
_____
_____
_____
_____
_____
_____
_____
_____
_____
_____
_____
_____
_____
_____
_____
_____
_____
_____

LAST WORD IN ("Best Moment of Today" – "My Final Thought on Today" – "NOPE!, Never Again"):

$h!+ happeneds

☐ **Another Great Day! Stop catching sour feelings and enjoy life's sweetness. "I Love Me"**

Driving

Rage can't persist with happiness. It's impossible to have road rage with a positive attitude. Feeling good on the inside always shines through to the outside. The feeling you have after listening to your favorite song, joke, motivational speech, or radio station before exiting the vehicle always shines through. The smile and confidence you gain after viewing your favorite picture, quote, or spiritual scripture before exiting the vehicle always shines through.

through life

There's better in each new day; if you focus on it instead of the bad, that happens somedays. Pass the wealth. Pay your happiness forward. Nobody can own your smile. One of the best ways to change the negative attitude of most people is to overpower their presence with positive energy and a smile.

while being mindful

What you considered non-stop complaining in your last relationship will be termed "nagging" in the next. It's the same "YOU" but different person complaining.

How about *you* do yourself a favor and answer these few questions:

1. Do you know what makes the difference in you being angered, flustered, or calm and in control?
2. Do you know why you don't like being or sharing your authentic self with others?
3. Do you know who's responsible for your daily joy and life appreciation?
4. Do you know who makes you happy or sad?
5. Do you know who's to answer for your right or wrong,
6. Do you know who suffer because of what you do or fail to do?
7. Do you know you?

Extra credit if you can understand any below (each worth 50%):

1. Do you know you?
2. Do you DO YOU?

FT GHAMBE

Woke-up _____ on _____/_____/_____ M T W T F S S   Hours of sleep ____

Sunny__ Cloudy__ Rainy__ Stormy__ Lightning__ Windy__ WTHail__ Snow__ WTMother Nature__

TODAY, I AM

☐	☐	☐	☐	☐	☐	STOP	☐	☐	☐	☐	☐	☐
GREAT	HOPEFUL	AWESOME	MINDFUL	BOLD	ENCOURAGED		GROUCHY	HURT	ANGRY	MAD	BELLIGERENT	ENRAGED
GOOD	HAPPY	ACTIVE	MOTIVATED	BRILLIANT	ENERGIZED		GUARDED	HATEFUL	ANNOYED	MOODY	BITTER	EXHAUSTED

TODAY, I AM GRATEFUL & EXCITED ABOUT:

_____

_____

_____

_____

_____

_____

_____

_____

_____

_____

_____

_____

_____

_____

_____

_____

_____

_____

_____

_____

_____

_____

_____

_____

_____

LAST WORD IN ("Best Moment of Today" – "My Final Thought on Today" – "NOPE!, Never Again"):

$h!+ happeneds

☐ **Another Great Day! Raise the roof. "I Love Me"**

Driving

Do you have auto insurance? Is insurance required to drive?
Does insurance cost too much, or will it cost you more when you're not insured?

through life

Do you have health or life insurance? Is life insurance for you or the ones you love?
Is the cost of insurance too much, or does it cost your loved ones more without it?

while being mindful

- Do you plan for the weather if it's going to storm tomorrow?
- Does insurance cost more than the hospital or funeral cost without insurance?
- Can your family afford you not having insurance?
- Don't do what society favors as the norm if it's abnormal to you.
- Funerals are big business and they're an indoctrinated exuberance fanfare for a person's flesh/body, shell, or vessel and have nothing to do with the spirit of a person and their memories that continue to flourish through the lives they touch. Cremation?
- Would you rent out a venue for $8-15,000 for friends and family members to eat, watch a play and not charge anyone? Never put your family too far out there in financial debt to impress many whom they've never seen or will ever see again for less than an hour. Stop boosting the pockets of others when it's your family pocket requiring or needing a boost while mourning and dealing your loss of life. A life loss that was a financial and emotional support loss.
- Lastly, don't take it for granted and think you won't ever get sick or die because we all do.

Death is inevitable but still no insurance or thereafter plan.

1. What are the types of life insurances available? Research what's the best cost and option.
2. What amount do you need to reduce or pay off medical, burial, cremation, mortgage, or sustain your loving family lifestyle or place of residence?
3. Who's the beneficiary? Is the beneficiary updated? Is the beneficiary aware of being documented?
4. What's not covered by your life insurance (preexisting health condition or cause of death).
5. Where's the insurance documentation for family access?
6. Why does everybody choose to give their valuable time, flowers, or social media condolences when they're gone?

Is the insurance and funeral coverage payment plan too expensive (cremation/burial)?

1. How many alcoholic beverages do you purchase monthly?
2. How much do you spend playing the lottery or gambling each month?
3. How much do you spend on shoes and clothing monthly?
4. How many months' payment worth was a recent luxury purchase, trip, or extravagant party?
5. How much do you pay for the streaming services monthly?
6. How much do you eat out weekly or monthly?
7. How much insurance could you afford after re-allocating your wants and vices payments?

Driving through life, while being mindful that

Woke-up _____ on ____/____/_____   M T W T F S S   Hours of sleep ____

Sunny__ Cloudy__ Rainy__ Stormy__ Lightning__ Windy__ WTHail__ Snow__ WTMother Nature__

TODAY, I AM

☐	☐	☐	☐	☐	☐	🛑 STOP	☐	☐	☐	☐	☐	☐
GREAT	HOPEFUL	AWESOME	MINDFUL	BOLD	ENCOURAGED		GROUCHY	HURT	ANGRY	MAD	BELLIGERENT	ENRAGED
GOOD	HAPPY	ACTIVE	MOTIVATED	BRILLIANT	ENERGIZED		GUARDED	HATEFUL	ANNOYED	MOODY	BITTER	EXHAUSTED

TODAY, I AM GRATEFUL & EXCITED ABOUT:

_____

_____

_____

_____

LAST WORD IN ("Best Moment of Today" – "My Final Thought on Today" – "NOPE!, Never Again"):

$h!+ happeneds

☐ **Another Great Day! I control the peace around me. "I Love Me"**

Driving
- There are three ways to lose your driving privileges- Suspension, Revoked, and Cancellation.
- Driving has grave consequences, and unlike a video driving game, real life doesn't have a restart button. For some drivers, it takes the loss of their driving privilege to appreciate having the right to drive, and for repetitive offenders, it takes the loss of their freedom or someone's life.

through life
- There are three ways to lose yourself- Mind, Body, and Soul.
- Life is profound. For some, it takes the loss of someone or something they value to appreciate life and do right.

while being mindful

A coach or an experienced person can coach, train, mentor, teach, guide, instruct, and demonstrate, but it's up to you to listen, learn, follow, and execute.

It's crucial, so get it right.
The best way to gain experience is by doing.

0001 ANOTHER ONE!

Woke-up _____ on ____/____/____ M T W T F S S Hours of sleep ____

Sunny__ Cloudy__ Rainy__ Stormy__ Lightning__ Windy__ WTHail__ Snow__ WTMother Nature__

TODAY, I AM

☐ ☐ ☐ ☐ ☐ ☐ **STOP** ☐ ☐ ☐ ☐ ☐ ☐
GREAT HOPEFUL AWESOME MINDFUL BOLD ENCOURAGED GROUCHY HURT ANGRY MAD BELLIGERENT ENRAGED

GOOD HAPPY ACTIVE MOTIVATED BRILLIANT ENERGIZED GUARDED HATEFUL ANNOYED MOODY BITTER EXHAUSTED

TODAY, I AM GRATEFUL & EXCITED ABOUT:

_____

_____
_____
_____
_____
_____
_____
_____
_____
_____
_____
_____
_____
_____
_____
_____
_____
_____
_____
_____
_____
_____
_____
_____
_____

LAST WORD IN ("Best Moment of Today" – "My Final Thought on Today" – "NOPE!, Never Again"):

$h!+ happeneds

☐ **Make A Note. It's Another Great Day to Learn Something New! "I Love Me"**

Are your rights being violated where you reside, pay taxes, and boost the economy. Research your state's legal rights (varies) and have an awareness and acknowledgment of your rights.

☐ Legal rights. <u>Reminder</u>: There are subject matter legal eagles (lawyers) who exist to assist.

☐ A right to life, liberty, and the pursuit of happiness.

☐ A right to peace and calmness.

☐ A right to de-escalation before escalation.

☐ A right to equal and fair treatment.

☐ A right to remain silent. A right against self-incrimination

☐ A right to choose.

☐ A right to remain inside my vehicle or home w/o probable cause for me to exit

☐ I have the right to only allow you in my place of residency with a signed judicial warrant listing my address and areas of search.

☐ A right to observe where to search.

☐ A right not to consent to a search of myself, my vehicle, or my belongings.

☐ A right to a phone call.

☐ A video right my interaction with you.

☐ A right to a phone call to a lawyer with privacy.

☐ A right to legal counsel.

☐ A right not to sign any document other than a traffic ticket without the council present.

☐ A right to not show ID unless operating a vehicle or probable cause to believe a law is violated.

☐ A right to refuse a breath, blood, or urine test (Automatic suspension?).

☐ A right to a reasonable expectation of professionalism and privacy.

☐ A right to file a lawsuit or complaint if my rights have been violated.

☐ A right to be released on your accord if of legal age.

☐ A right to say no, stop, or refuse further…

☐ A right to evidence material of my guilt or innocence.

☐ A right to plea to federal agencies records or information.

☐ **A right to liberty, freedom, opportunity, justice, and citizenship EQUAL TO ALL.**

Driving through life, while being mindful that

Woke-up _____ on ____/____/_____   M T W T F S S   Hours of sleep ____

Sunny__ Cloudy__ Rainy__ Stormy__ Lightning__ Windy__ WTHail__ Snow__ WTMother Nature__

TODAY, I AM

☐ GREAT ☐ HOPEFUL ☐ AWESOME ☐ MINDFUL ☐ BOLD ☐ ENCOURAGED **STOP** ☐ GROUCHY ☐ HURT ☐ ANGRY ☐ MAD ☐ BELLIGERENT ☐ ENRAGED

GOOD   HAPPY   ACTIVE   MOTIVATED BRILLIANT ENERGIZED | GUARDED HATEFUL ANNOYED MOODY   BITTER EXHAUSTED

TODAY, I AM GRATEFUL & EXCITED ABOUT:

_____

_____
_____
_____
_____
_____
_____
_____
_____
_____
_____
_____
_____
_____
_____
_____
_____
_____
_____
_____
_____
_____
_____
_____

LAST WORD IN ("Best Moment of Today" – "My Final Thought on Today" – "NOPE!, Never Again"):

$h!+ happeneds

☐ **Good morning sunshine! Another Great Day! "I Love Me"**

Driving
The use of a vehicle horn is to alert more than be an annoyance; so, use it and listen to it.

through life
It's maturity when you know when to speak up, speak out or listen only.
- Speak up against injustice, racism, inequality, intolerance, and loss of a human right.
- Speak out for spotlighting, protesting injustice, racism, inequality, intolerance, and loss of someone's human right. A bias bill toward or against any race is a bias to all races.
- Listen only. Stop responding to someone who is bluntly racist toward you and who'll never agree that there is a systematic system of injustice, racism, inequality, intolerance, and human rights violation toward non-whites. Like, IHAAATE People.

while being mindful
<u>Selective hearing</u> or <u>Intentional disregard</u>. Listening to what is said is as important as what is being said.

Get up, Stand up
For the States of America and its people to be united, Americans must know of the United States of America's systematic racial history and construction by slavery, sale of human beings, beating, raping, family separation, cotton industry, lynching, biased institutions, legal injustice, Black Americans military sacrifice and contribution, educational inequalities, blind-eye to racial mobs, whites-only signs, limited resources, blacks inventions, non-whites food and cultural appropriation and procreation, profit sharing penal system, Jim Crow, inadequate and inappropriate medical treatment and testing, sport and entertainment exploitation, housing and finacial & financial-gap, Black Wall Street tragedy and injustice, legal oppression, WHAAATE Washing and Flight, and the use of hidden federally funded spies or opportunists (OKAYE, RHACISTS, and IHAAATE People).

Why are some Americans so patriotic for Americans competing against other nations in competitions but not as vigorously when supporting one another. Who's less American than I?
You are less than if you haven't accumulated the same bigness and opulence.
You are less than because another person identified as different or less than you succeeded you.
You are less than if you don't believe in the religion I believe.
You are less than if your child doesn't attend a school in my district.
You are less than if you can't provide what I can afford to provide.
You are less than if you're a subtitle American (_____-American).
You are less than if you don't speak English or what I deem as correct or proper English.
You are less than if you don't express your patriotism (biggest flag) more than I or we?
You are less than if you can't afford the same mortgaged square footage or vehicle on loan?
You are less than because your skin color differs from mine.
You are less than because your action in the media matches what I was raised to believe of you.
You are less than me because you were not born here?
You are less than because you're not doing as I or we are doing in politics, wealth, or bigotry?
You are less than because you never wear, display, voice, or portray you're a Proud American.

Driving through life, while being mindful that

Woke-up _____ on ____/_____/_____   M T W T F S S   Hours of sleep ____

Sunny__ Cloudy__ Rainy__ Stormy__   Lightning__ Windy__ WTHail__ Snow__ WTMother Nature__

TODAY, I AM

☐	☐	☐	☐	☐	☐	🛑	☐	☐	☐	☐	☐	☐
GREAT	HOPEFUL	AWESOME	MINDFUL	BOLD	ENCOURAGED		GROUCHY	HURT	ANGRY	MAD	BELLIGERENT	ENRAGED
GOOD	HAPPY	ACTIVE	MOTIVATED	BRILLIANT	ENERGIZED		GUARDED	HATEFUL	ANNOYED	MOODY	BITTER	EXHAUSTED

TODAY, I AM GRATEFUL & EXCITED ABOUT:

_____

_____
_____
_____
_____
_____
_____
_____
_____
_____
_____
_____
_____
_____
_____
_____
_____
_____
_____
_____
_____
_____
_____
_____

LAST WORD IN ("Best Moment of Today" – "My Final Thought on Today" – "NOPE!, Never Again"):

$h!+ happeneds

☐ **Another Entertaining Day! Yes, it's in the air somedays. "JJ" I can smell it. "I Love Me"** Past CRT in the entertainment and media industry caused a race of people to hate, disguise, and stifle their gifted hair texture with straight hair. Even in 2023, WHAAATEs are using policies to stifle and make ethnic hairstyle shameful. How many non-white natural hairstyles (course & curly) are championed on your favorite news, entertainment show, or award ceremony? Why not? **African Descendants**-Stop stifling your life and stop stifling your natural hair and let both breathe. The fear of black's embracing naturalness is an economic fear of disrupting the beauty industry that finances economies worldwide. Who defined what's beautiful? Whose definition defines you?

It's not the theory of CRT to blackwash the past or make WHAAATEs or whites feel any guilt for America's racist past. CRT is to assist in removing the WHAAATE Wash of America's systematic racist history and awaken descendants of those enslaved people to see themselves clearly and appreciate their worth. There's no future without a past. There's no trees, vegetation, or beautiful flowers blooming without a seed planted, rooted, and nutrients.

In the past, WHAAATE separatists justified their implementation of WHAAATE Critical Reckoning Theory, which made sure history books gave a one-sided view of non-whites as a minority and lesser than others while highlighting and glorifying WHAAATEs as superiors and heroes. Systematically educating (indoctrinating) all categorized (separative labeled non-whites to believe that the WHAAATE race discovered, invented, signed, established, incorporated, served, died for, created law, gave rights, and built everything (roads, railroad, industries, and wealth) for the colonies. In the present, WHAAATE Critical Reckoning Truthfulness isn't justified because it still brings about a colorless or unbiased point of view that's not championed by whites, non-whites, or right the wrong of Africans being enslaved (involuntary?), Indian genocide (tricked, encamped/reservation and sickened), or Asians encampment (trafficked for cheap labor) without cause. How can a nation be inclusive with growth and prosperity if the descendants of non-white are experiencing the same conservative righteousness and citizen inequalities as their ancestors?
1. Why does an African descendant's request for their ancestor's importance and brilliance be included in any nation's building narrative bring about hatred toward today's WHAAATEs?
2. Why's a black person's inclusion in commercials and superhero movies too much or too woke but not too much when WHAAATE Washing racism omitted and limited black representation in past entertainment roles? More non-whites appearing on the shows representing their neighborhoods, cultures, or environment shouldn't receive backlash or outrage. The outrage is the change being noticeable instead of it being the norm. Past CRT in the entertainment industry caused American descendants of Africa to believe Egyptians were WHAAATEs and not African. African were portrayed more afraid of the African wild than Tarzan. Tarzan was portrayed to be more accepted in the African jungle than Africans.
3. Should we be referencing racism as a part of the past if it's still existing? How does a descendant deflect or negate their past ancestor's racism but won't shun the same ideology that continues today by the same ideology of racist family members, or their associated group?

WHAAATE!
Don't get caught up on any WHAAATE's hateful book narrative of blacks being an enslaved and unwelcomed import to America more than being known as being important (Import American National Treasure). We're all important and we're all part of America's past, present, and future.

Woke-up _____ on _____/_____/_____   M T W T F S S   Hours of sleep _____

Sunny__ Cloudy__ Rainy__ Stormy__ Lightning__ Windy__ WTHail__ Snow__ WTMother Nature__

TODAY, I AM

☐ GREAT / GOOD
☐ HOPEFUL / HAPPY
☐ AWESOME / ACTIVE
☐ MINDFUL / MOTIVATED
☐ BOLD / BRILLIANT
☐ ENCOURAGED / ENERGIZED

STOP

☐ GROUCHY / GUARDED
☐ HURT / HATEFUL
☐ ANGRY / ANNOYED
☐ MAD / MOODY
☐ BELLIGERENT / BITTER
☐ ENRAGED / EXHAUSTED

TODAY, I AM GRATEFUL & EXCITED ABOUT:

_____
_____
_____
_____
_____
_____
_____
_____
_____
_____
_____
_____
_____
_____
_____
_____
_____
_____
_____
_____
_____
_____

LAST WORD IN ("Best Moment of Today" – "My Final Thought on Today" – "NOPE!, Never Again"):

$h!+ happeneds

■■■■■■

☐ **Another Great Day! This is how it's going down. "I Love Me"**

~~America's History:~~
There's the history of WHAAATE men's oppression, silencing, and impoverishing Whites (*see as defined*) and non-whites (African, Caribbean, Hawaiian, Indians/Native Americans, and other indigenous people) with the assistance of RHACISTS (as defined).

There's a history of WHAAATE ~~Sup!@#m%$+~~ oppression of non-whites with an undertone of WHAAATE Christian nationalism (WHAAATE Lives Matter) but with an overtone and fearmongering at Whites to overshadow with All Lives Matter, with outlandish agenda as "WHAAATE along with Whites are being oppressed, silenced, and impoverished to second class to non-whites." WHAAATE's want all Whites to fear losing their race majority and power in the future. A WHAAATE belief: America's existence and dominance was and is only due to WHAAATE and Whites being united in an agreement. **Whites, please don't fall for the bipartisan trickery and fearmongering of the WHAAATE S**ystematic **H**istorian's **I**nferiority **T**actics. **(caution)** Please be cautious of race being used to spread purposeful misinformation of 'Whites American's losing their jobs, identity, or white majority by year ____? Who's still making changes to maintain steadfast control over its citizens, by changing laws to nullify citizen's votes, and manipulate boundaries to limit voting power of non-white citizens since 1776? **Who's...?**

☐ The majority within the state and federal government, the majority within the three branches of government?
☐ The governor majority controlling enormous government funds and contracts?
☐ The owner of the gas & electric power grid through all states
☐ The majority pushing forward bills to take away citizens' rights?
☐ Of television, radio, streaming services, and media empires and how the news is spun?
☐ Receives the most support within our farming industry.
☐ The majority within SCOTUS (of the people)?
☐ Over the religions that missionaries were sent out to convert natives away from their deity, spirituality, and beliefs?
☐ The majority who sustain or change laws, policies, and rights?
☐ Over books, movies, and music publishing and distribution?
☐ Over coffers with billions of non-taxed dollars of non-profit organization?
☐ In ownership of pharmaceutical companies?
☐ In ownership of oil refineries and distribution?
☐ In ownership of private prisons and detention centers?
☐ In ownership and manufacturing of vehicles?
☐ In clothing, food, apparel, real estate, tech, groceries, and medical marijuana ownership?
☐ Of land ownership, power, fame, employment, lotteries, finances, and wealth?
☐ Of the largest conglomerates with U.S. business (not run or lead)?
☐ Over the social platforms used for livelihood and connections.

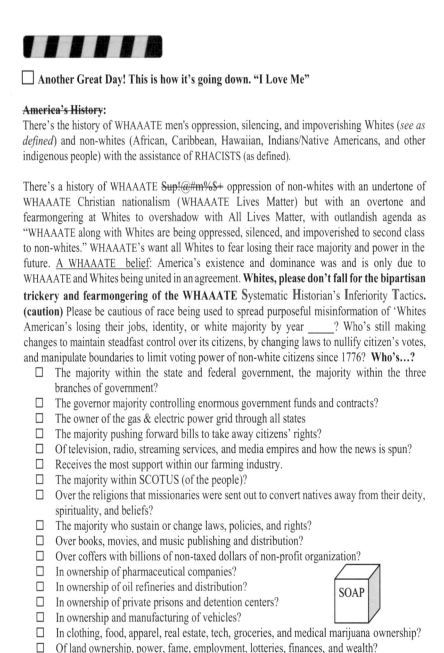

WHAAATE Minute! Whose lineage maintains steadfast control of being succeeded into the above all-powerful financial structures. A structure created and implemented by monarchs, enslavers, bankers, millionaires, and political leaders who were WHAAATE men? Equal is top to bottom, not bottom to middle. Who's still fighting for citizenship recognition and voting equality and fairness?

FT GHAMBE

Woke-up _____ on _____/_____/_____   M T W T F S S   Hours of sleep ____

Sunny__ Cloudy__ Rainy__ Stormy__   Lightning__ Windy__ WTHail__ Snow__ WTMother Nature__

TODAY, I AM

☐	☐	☐	☐	☐	☐	**STOP**	☐	☐	☐	☐	☐	☐
GREAT	HOPEFUL	AWESOME	MINDFUL	BOLD	ENCOURAGED		GROUCHY	HURT	ANGRY	MAD	BELLIGERENT	ENRAGED
GOOD	HAPPY	ACTIVE	MOTIVATED	BRILLIANT	ENERGIZED		GUARDED	HATEFUL	ANNOYED	MOODY	BITTER	EXHAUSTED

TODAY, I AM GRATEFUL & EXCITED ABOUT:

_____

_____

_____

_____

_____

_____

_____

_____

_____

_____

_____

_____

_____

_____

_____

_____

_____

_____

_____

_____

_____

_____

_____

_____

LAST WORD IN ("Best Moment of Today" – "My Final Thought on Today" – "NOPE!, Never Again"):

$h!+ happeneds

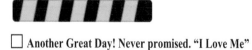

☐ **Another Great Day! Never promised. "I Love Me"**

Driving

One MPH above a post speed limit is over the speed limit, but luckily not all traffic enforcers ticket you for going slightly over the post speed limit.

through life

Anything you do or say can be misinterpreted, but luckily for you, some will interpret and understand it just as you meant.

while being mindful

Age Limit: the legal maximum age at which an individual may speak on having a clue about life.

1. **14-17 Age limit**: A teen who thinks they know more than adults but have no clue.
2. **18-21 Age limit**: A young adult who believes they know more because they're considered an adult but comes to learn they're still missing a lot of information and without a clue.
3. **21-24 Age limit**: An adult who understands adult consequences more and slightly begins to recognize and appreciate some past adults trying to inform them that they didn't have a clue.
4. **25-28 Age limit**: An adult who has gained the knowledge to know life lessons will never stop and is fully aware that clues differ individually.
5. **28 to numerous experiences limit**: An adult who shakes their head east and west whenever they hear or witness the younger generation doing what they think they know but without a clue.
   a. An adult who attempts to share knowledge with the younger generation but isn't believed because they're now considered old and out of touch.

Love Limit: a love pace sustained at which someone does everything in the ability to remain in a particular loving relationship. Most individuals exceed their love limits for their loved ones due to an unhealthy or risky lifestyles (excessive, careless, or reckless). A lifestyle that limits their time to live and love.

Excessive Love Limit violations (watch out for loves traps)**:**
1. Excessive & Reckless Driving Speeds
2. Excessive Alcohol Use, Misue, and Abuse
3. Excessive Drug (prescriptions & recreational included) Use, Misue, and Abuse
4. Domestic & Gun Violence
5. Crimes Against Others

Are you maintaining or exceeding your love expectations?
1. Are you doing everything possible to be around with your family, to love and be loved?
2. Are you doing your part in appreciating and extending your loved life? *Daily gratitude helps*
3. Will the love in your future be limited or limitless?

Woke-up _____ on _____/_____/_____   M T W T F S S   Hours of sleep _____

Sunny__ Cloudy__ Rainy__ Stormy__ Lightning__ Windy__ WTHail__ Snow__ WTMother Nature__

TODAY, I AM

☐ GREAT   ☐ HOPEFUL   ☐ AWESOME   ☐ MINDFUL   ☐ BOLD   ☐ ENCOURAGED   **STOP**   ☐ GROUCHY   ☐ HURT   ☐ ANGRY   ☐ MAD   ☐ BELLIGERENT   ☐ ENRAGED

GOOD   HAPPY   ACTIVE   MOTIVATED   BRILLIANT   ENERGIZED | GUARDED   HATEFUL   ANNOYED   MOODY   BITTER   EXHAUSTED

TODAY, I AM GRATEFUL & EXCITED ABOUT:

_____

_____

_____

_____

_____

_____

_____

_____

_____

_____

_____

_____

_____

_____

_____

_____

_____

_____

_____

_____

_____

_____

_____

LAST WORD IN ("Best Moment of Today" – "My Final Thought on Today" – "NOPE!, Never Again"):

$h!+ happeneds

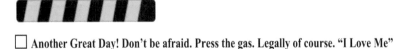

☐ **Another Great Day! Don't be afraid. Press the gas. Legally of course. "I Love Me"**

Driving

Be prepared to drive on the opposite side of the road in some countries. Some countries have no intention of changing their way of driving, so you either adapt to their way of driving, ride it out everywhere (TAXI!) or "Walk It Out."

through life

Be prepared to meet individual(s) who don't know you but choose to hate you because they were raised to view and treat you as their opposite. Some individuals have no intentions or will ever see themselves changing, and you must mentally prepare yourself never to react without pause, to never mirror their way of thinking or living.

while being mindful

Racists are raised to believe in race labels and are convinced there is a human being difference by one's melanin type/amount (skin tone) or outer appearance alone. A Racist's goal is to try to make you respond indifferent publicly, to assist in getting more to believe there's a difference. Racism must have leader's and followers to exist and an opposing side to thrive. Stop assisting a racist's public display or survival with your time and energy over words. **Reminder:** They have a problem with you. You don't.

Racism is taught. A racist teacher + student. A racist parent + child. A racist group + poor vs middle vs 3%

1. How does a racist know how to mistreat another human they've never encountered?
2. How does a racist know what racist words, comments, and symbolization causes reactions?
3. How does an individual against racism know to be angered by a racist's word or display?
4. Who developed and implemented what derogatory words, terms, flags, as inflammatory and racist for each race category?
5. On GP, how was racial and ethnic categorization of humans infused in America's structure?

Racism is lucrative.

1. It's lucrative to be a lead voice within racists rhetoric or be silent about its usage or purpose (especially for political donations). Why do the politicians who illuminate race raise the most?
2. It's more lucrative to be the lead voice against a racist, racist organization or own race.
3. It's lucrative to incite and festers racism by politicians. "They are coming for your livelihood."
4. It's lucrative to incite, fester, or be in the grey area (never shuns) of divisive racial politicizing within a party or supporter's ideology or actions (far-far-far left or right)
5. It's lucrative to media conglomerates who reap the financial rewards of ads fueling racial and political divisiveness:
   Politician: "I approve of this message." **Media Network (owners, board members, and shareholders):** "Thank you, we approve your PAID messages."
   Constituents: What happens to my campaign donations? Can I receive a donation refund and transfer to another party member? Where's the leftover dollars? Can we see the disbursement of our donations? What Political Action Committee (PAC) received my donations? Can my donations be used for personal use once moved? Where does the money end? Political or Paid **on GP, checkout .gov:** Federal Election Commission and Committee on Ethics

Woke-up _____ on ____/____/_____   M T W T F S S   Hours of sleep ____

Sunny__ Cloudy__ Rainy__ Stormy__ Lightning__ Windy__ WTHail__ Snow__ WTMother Nature__

TODAY, I AM

☐	☐	☐	☐	☐	☐	STOP	☐	☐	☐	☐	☐	☐
GREAT	HOPEFUL	AWESOME	MINDFUL	BOLD	ENCOURAGED		GROUCHY	HURT	ANGRY	MAD	BELLIGERENT	ENRAGED
GOOD	HAPPY	ACTIVE	MOTIVATED	BRILLIANT	ENERGIZED		GUARDED	HATEFUL	ANNOYED	MOODY	BITTER	EXHAUSTED

TODAY, I AM GRATEFUL & EXCITED ABOUT:

_____

_____

_____

_____

_____

_____

_____

_____

_____

_____

_____

_____

_____

_____

_____

_____

_____

_____

_____

_____

_____

_____

_____

_____

LAST WORD IN ("Best Moment of Today" – "My Final Thought on Today" – "NOPE!, Never Again"):

$h!+ happeneds

☐ **Another Great Day!** Yes, it's a **BIG** deal. One of the biggest. **"I Love Me"**

Driving

Watch your lane! Don't be the inattentive driver in the right lane rear-ending a vehicle because you are concentrating on the vehicles going in the opposite direction.

through life

Know where you are going in life more than where everybody else is going.

while being mindful

Americans need some R&R time. <u>Repairation</u> & Reparations. Who do you think should be more open-minded about discussing repairation to implement a reparation action plan?

1. Who developed a race category before fortifying citizenship and entitlements?
2. Who established a hidden power and financial economic structure (less than vs poor vs rich) before (poor vs middle class vs almost rich vs rich vs wealth)?
3. Who created America's history and generations of students with unproven pass-down stories, tales, fabrications, beliefs, and assumptions without evidence or the other categorized citizens being allowed to speak or write about their history and humanity?
4. Who establish inequality in history books publications to make individuals of color appear lesser and against America's development before anyone could legally cry foul of unfairness and unequal race representation in America's history.
5. Whose agenda favors keeping many dependent on the government? Whose agenda benefits keeping many uneducated and limited by some media? Who agenda favors all being rule under one religion and justify an authoritarian government and dictatorship.
6. Who hid cowardly behind WHAAATE sheets before purposely transitioning behind badges, desks of board rooms, financial institutions, courtrooms, and political offices.
7. Who refine tax law for millionaires to become billionaires and onward to trillionaires?
8. Who's politically justified in bringing forth laws limiting videoing and protecting lone (surviving) police officers of an incident involving a citizen?
9. Who looks the other way when an officer yells "Stop Resisting" or something aloud to favor officer on audio for something that goes terribly wrong due to an officer's action?
10. Who's involved in political donations and quid pro quo yea or nay vote agreements?
11. Who established a political agenda to limit and distress citizens to make them favor a campaigning political government savior with false promises? Who promise pharmaceutical conglomerate with government purchase order agreement before vaccine implementation and mandates.
12. Who favor creating a new district because of population changes but are really concerned that an ethnic population increase, or change will hinder or takeaway votes.
13. Who's comfortable with a few mayors being the first of a race or gender elected but not for senator?
14. Who's comfortable with product or channel provider but not the distributor or owner?
15. Who benefits and who is shielded if a first elected race or gender mayor is embroiled in a scandal and faulted for state issues for laws and policies previously passed?
16. Who's guaranteed monetary association and favors for life by sponsoring big business.

Driving through life, while being mindful that

Woke-up _____ on ____/____/_____   M T W T F S S   Hours of sleep ____

Sunny_   Cloudy_   Rainy_   Stormy_   Lightning_   Windy_   WTHail_   Snow_ WTMother Nature__

TODAY, I AM

☐   ☐   ☐   ☐   ☐   ☐   **STOP**   ☐   ☐   ☐   ☐   ☐   ☐

GREAT   HOPEFUL   AWESOME   MINDFUL   BOLD   ENCOURAGED   GROUCHY   HURT   ANGRY   MAD   BELLIGERENT   ENRAGED

GOOD   HAPPY   ACTIVE   MOTIVATED   BRILLIANT   ENERGIZED   GUARDED   HATEFUL   ANNOYED   MOODY   BITTER   EXHAUSTED

TODAY, I AM GRATEFUL & EXCITED ABOUT:

_____

_____

_____

_____

_____

_____

_____

_____

_____

_____

_____

_____

_____

_____

_____

_____

_____

_____

_____

_____

_____

_____

_____

_____

_____

LAST WORD IN ("Best Moment of Today" – "My Final Thought on Today" – "NOPE!, Never Again"):

$h!+ happeneds

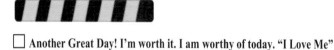

☐ **Another Great Day! I'm worth it. I am worthy of today. "I Love Me"**

Driving

The stimulants or depressants you use for pain, coping, or recreational use while operating a vehicle will be temporary. Still, the pain, destructions, or fatality you caused due to being under the influence are permanent.

through life

The way drugs and alcohol make you feel is always temporary, so only seek a safer and more conducive euphoria.

while being mindful

Life is the actual high because it's what every person seeks and hopes they still have after any temporary substance induced high or state of mind. Only seek life's conducive and euphoric high.

What's considered life's conducive and euphoric moment: a child's birth, baby first cry, baby first step, first picture, first school project, child hugging back, hello, child uttering momma or dadda, grandparent, passing to higher education grade, sports accomplishment, sports team win, a powerful speech, making the team, graduation day, college acceptance, hearing" proud of you", basic training graduation, first home, first time returning home, promotion, wedding day, driving, pet missing you, first job/paycheck, being recognized, receiving an award for your talent, a recent/past "Thank You!", thanks for volunteering, thank you for your service, thank you for listening, thanks for your time, mentorship, being appreciated, rescuing/saving a life, being saved, donor, donating, your hired, needed hug, fond memory of a love one, being loved, favorite cuisine the first time, freedom, citizenship, military/career promotion, marriage, divorce uncontested/final, sobriety, best movie/concert ever, funny joke, short trip, vacation, a kiss, first love, first time you saw your partner, particular song, or hearing and experiencing "I LOVE YOU!".

Woke-up _____ on ____/____/____ M T W T F S S Hours of sleep ____

Sunny__ Cloudy__ Rainy__ Stormy__ Lightning__ Windy__ WTHail__ Snow__ WTMother Nature__

TODAY, I AM

☐	☐	☐	☐	☐	☐	STOP	☐	☐	☐	☐	☐	☐
GREAT	HOPEFUL	AWESOME	MINDFUL	BOLD	ENCOURAGED		GROUCHY	HURT	ANGRY	MAD	BELLIGERENT	ENRAGED
GOOD	HAPPY	ACTIVE	MOTIVATED	BRILLIANT	ENERGIZED		GUARDED	HATEFUL	ANNOYED	MOODY	BITTER	EXHAUSTED

TODAY, I AM GRATEFUL & EXCITED ABOUT:

_____

_____
_____
_____
_____
_____
_____
_____
_____
_____
_____
_____
_____
_____
_____
_____
_____
_____
_____
_____
_____
_____
_____
_____

LAST WORD IN ("Best Moment of Today" – "My Final Thought on Today" – "NOPE!, Never Again"):

$h!+ happeneds

☐ **Another Great Day! My Way. "I Love Me"**

Driving

It's hard to blame another vehicle if you're the only vehicle involved in a single-vehicle collision.

through life

Is it plausible and quick to blame a book, movie, song, or video game to excuse someone committing a heinous criminal act when a million others have read, watched, listened, or played the same without an issue? How about allowing some individuals to own their part in their grown ass actions.

while being mindful

Some grown ass decisions and choices will lead to grown ass repercussion. Everyone's life is leased to determine age; so, never try to take full ownership of another's life who feel they own it outright. Let them own their own $h!+. It's the only reality for a few. Help, guide, plead, insist, pray, or admit until your livelihood is at risk of being the same or worse.

When their actions begin to destroy your sanity, health, livelihood, or being, you must let them:

- Own their problem.
- Own their addiction.
- Own their lapse in judgment.
- Own their crime.
- Own their socialization stubbornness, misjudgment and being charged as an accessory.
- Own their part throughout whatever shenanigans or $h!+ storm they created and inflicted on themselves.

*Help can only go so far with some because it's a heavy burden to carry. Seek others to assist in carry the weight or the professionals who lift heavy daily.

Woke-up _____ on ____/____/____ M T W T F S S   Hours of sleep ____

Sunny__ Cloudy__ Rainy__ Stormy__ Lightning__ Windy__ WTHail__ Snow__ WTMother Nature__

TODAY, I AM

☐	☐	☐	☐	☐	☐	🛑	☐	☐	☐	☐	☐	☐
GREAT	HOPEFUL	AWESOME	MINDFUL	BOLD	ENCOURAGED		GROUCHY	HURT	ANGRY	MAD	BELLIGERENT	ENRAGED
GOOD	HAPPY	ACTIVE	MOTIVATED	BRILLIANT	ENERGIZED		GUARDED	HATEFUL	ANNOYED	MOODY	BITTER	EXHAUSTED

TODAY, I AM GRATEFUL & EXCITED ABOUT:

_____

_____

_____

_____

_____

_____

_____

_____

_____

_____

_____

_____

_____

_____

_____

_____

_____

_____

_____

_____

_____

_____

_____

LAST WORD IN ("Best Moment of Today" – "My Final Thought on Today" – "NOPE!, Never Again"):

_____

$h!+ happeneds

☐ **Another Great Day! I am so proud of me. "I Love Me"**

Driving

> Don't allow your like or dislike of your first vehicle to dictate the selection preference of your future make, model, or type of vehicle, or you could miss out on the perfect vehicle for you. It would not be a true statement to say you favor driving a sedan over a pickup truck or SUV, but you have only driven a sedan and have never been in a truck or SUV.

through life

> It would be a false statement to say you hate an individual if you have never met them personally. Never shortchange yourself in meeting a great person or shortchange them from knowing you to be a great person by another's assumption, misconception, or unproven truth.

while being mindful

> One lousy person is one lousy person. There's a mixture of good and bad people in the world, and it's prejudiced to label any race, group, or nation as all bad because one or a few of those bad people associated happen to be categorized as….

Excluding "them downstairs" in disparity and hate.

The Hateful Extremist Members **(THEM):** THEM who are still against all citizens being UNITED with equal rights to liberty, freedom, opportunity, justice, and citizenship.

Woke-up _____ on ____/_____/_____   M T W T F S S   Hours of sleep ____

Sunny__ Cloudy__ Rainy__ Stormy__ Lightning__ Windy__ WTHail__ Snow__ WTMother Nature__

TODAY, I AM

☐	☐	☐	☐	☐	☐	STOP	☐	☐	☐	☐	☐	☐
GREAT	HOPEFUL	AWESOME	MINDFUL	BOLD	ENCOURAGED		GROUCHY	HURT	ANGRY	MAD	BELLIGERENT	ENRAGED
GOOD	HAPPY	ACTIVE	MOTIVATED	BRILLIANT	ENERGIZED		GUARDED	HATEFUL	ANNOYED	MOODY	BITTER	EXHAUSTED

TODAY, I AM GRATEFUL & EXCITED ABOUT:

_____

_____
_____
_____
_____
_____
_____
_____
_____
_____
_____
_____
_____
_____
_____
_____
_____
_____
_____
_____
_____
_____
_____
_____

LAST WORD IN ("Best Moment of Today" – "My Final Thought on Today" – "NOPE!, Never Again"):

$h!+ happeneds

☐ **Another Great Day! My favorite day once again. Another day for me. "I Love Me"**

Driving

How sure are you that the vehicle you're driving or riding in doesn't have illegal baggage or criminal evidence in the trunk or cab of the vehicle? Do you know what's in any of your passenger's possession that's occupying your vehicle while you're awaiting a police officer K-9-unit approach during a traffic stop?

through life

Should you remain loyal to someone that isn't loyal to you?

How confident are you of the associates you surround yourself with and what they've thrust in your surroundings? It's in your best interest to distinguish who you consider a friend, associate, or passerby before you are given an acquaintance, accessory, or co-conspirator title.

while being mindful

Make changes in your health, finances, education, relations, or associations before it's too late. It's easier to go from uncomfortable to comfortable than the opposite.

Quick life-changing scenario

You are facing five and one possible (not a game of spades).

You are out with 5 friends. You are sitting in the vehicle with another friend talking. One friend is out pumping gas. Two friends enter the store but suddenly both are running to get in vehicle and both yells "DRIVE! As you travel down the road; both are boasting about the money and items they just grabbed (stole). You are now in a vehicle with two individuals who has no respect for 3 other lives. Next, blue lights are flashing and suddenly you're all surrounded by several officers with weapons drawn. Everyone's life is at stake. Luckily (somewhat), everyone is arrested and taken in without harm. Everyone is facing 5+ years possible. Everyone knows the individual responsible. After the Miranda Rights have been read:

1. Who's going to waive their rights, confess, or remain silent?

2. Who's going to be loyal to friendship, family, or themselves?

3. Who's going down?

4. Who's going to take care of you or your family while you are in jail?

5. Who's going to put funds in your jail account. Will it be a sufficient apology for your demise?

6. Who's going to hire you with a criminal record after being released with a resume with 3–5+ years gap of non-employment (life missing/omitted)? It's a temporary job if you lie about it.

7. Some friends may say a loyal friend will never sugarcoat something from them, but many friends don't "have a clue" of their friend's preference and love of sweets or know their friend only considered them an associate, never a friend. **Loyal & Locked-Up or Lesson Learned.**

Driving through life, while being mindful that

Woke-up _____ on _____/_____/_____   M T W T F S S   Hours of sleep ____

Sunny__ Cloudy__ Rainy__ Stormy__ Lightning__ Windy__ WTHail__ Snow__ WTMother Nature__

TODAY, I AM

☐ GREAT   ☐ HOPEFUL   ☐ AWESOME   ☐ MINDFUL   ☐ BOLD   ☐ ENCOURAGED   🛑   ☐ GROUCHY   ☐ HURT   ☐ ANGRY   ☐ MAD   ☐ BELLIGERENT   ☐ ENRAGED

GOOD   HAPPY   ACTIVE   MOTIVATED   BRILLIANT   ENERGIZED | GUARDED   HATEFUL   ANNOYED   MOODY   BITTER   EXHAUSTED

TODAY, I AM GRATEFUL & EXCITED ABOUT:

_____

_____
_____
_____
_____
_____
_____
_____
_____
_____
_____
_____
_____
_____
_____
_____
_____
_____
_____
_____
_____
_____
_____
_____
_____

LAST WORD IN ("Best Moment of Today" – "My Final Thought on Today" – "NOPE!, Never Again"):

$h!+ happeneds

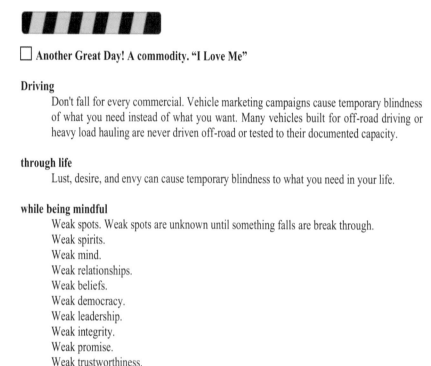

☐ **Another Great Day! A commodity. "I Love Me"**

Driving

Don't fall for every commercial. Vehicle marketing campaigns cause temporary blindness of what you need instead of what you want. Many vehicles built for off-road driving or heavy load hauling are never driven off-road or tested to their documented capacity.

through life

Lust, desire, and envy can cause temporary blindness to what you need in your life.

while being mindful

Weak spots. Weak spots are unknown until something falls are break through.
Weak spirits.
Weak mind.
Weak relationships.
Weak beliefs.
Weak democracy.
Weak leadership.
Weak integrity.
Weak promise.
Weak trustworthiness.
Weak security.

Weak: _____

Weak attractiveness visualizing

EYE CANDY can be a live cavity-causing sweetness. Finding love is like searching for dental care. A dentist you're comfortable with all aspect of dental care and a dental staff and service staff that compliments the practice (as front incisors and premolars compliment the molars).

Chew slowly:

1. First, Eye Candy gets caught in your eye.
2. You love the new candy, until the candy starts souring and has bitter taste after a while.
3. Eye candy immediately start tarnishing your love.
4. Without properly and thoroughly brushing away the eye candy the candy causes a decay in your love.
5. Attempting to floss and flush the love vigorously doesn't clear all the sweetness left behind.
6. Soon, the eye candy causes you to lose the rest of your love.
7. Next, you're forced to visit a professional to be fitted for control, love replacement, or removal of their remaining love.
8. Unfortunately, your too far gone, your remaining love must be removed, and some nerves are affected and must be numbed.
9. Immediately after the removal, you stop falling for the eye candy and vow never to mess with eye candy.
10. Even as time passes and you settle into your love removal, you're still leery and promised to stay away from all eye candy, but only time will tell if it's true. –"JJ"

Driving through life, while being mindful that

Woke-up _____ on _____/_____/_____   M T W T F S S   Hours of sleep ____

Sunny__ Cloudy__ Rainy__ Stormy__ Lightning__ Windy__ WTHail__ Snow__ WTMother Nature__

TODAY, I AM

☐ ☐ ☐ ☐ ☐ ☐ 🛑 ☐ ☐ ☐ ☐ ☐ ☐

GREAT	HOPEFUL	AWESOME	MINDFUL	BOLD	ENCOURAGED		GROUCHY	HURT	ANGRY	MAD	BELLIGERENT	ENRAGED
GOOD	HAPPY	ACTIVE	MOTIVATED	BRILLIANT	ENERGIZED		GUARDED	HATEFUL	ANNOYED	MOODY	BITTER	EXHAUSTED

TODAY, I AM GRATEFUL & EXCITED ABOUT:

_____

_____
_____
_____
_____
_____
_____
_____
_____
_____
_____
_____
_____
_____
_____
_____
_____
_____
_____
_____
_____
_____
_____
_____
_____
_____
_____

LAST WORD IN ("Best Moment of Today" – "My Final Thought on Today" – "NOPE!, Never Again"):

$h!+ happeneds

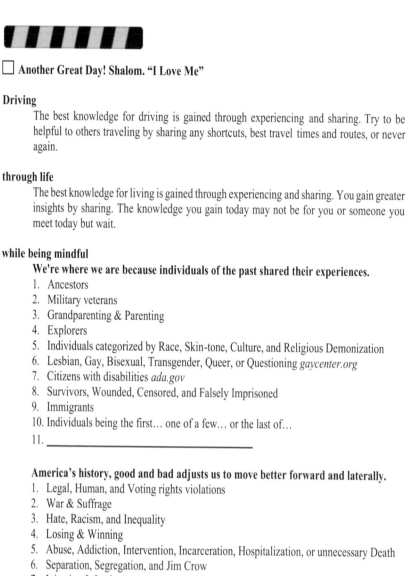

☐ **Another Great Day! Shalom. "I Love Me"**

Driving

The best knowledge for driving is gained through experiencing and sharing. Try to be helpful to others traveling by sharing any shortcuts, best travel times and routes, or never again.

through life

The best knowledge for living is gained through experiencing and sharing. You gain greater insights by sharing. The knowledge you gain today may not be for you or someone you meet today but wait.

while being mindful

We're where we are because individuals of the past shared their experiences.
1. Ancestors
2. Military veterans
3. Grandparenting & Parenting
4. Explorers
5. Individuals categorized by Race, Skin-tone, Culture, and Religious Demonization
6. Lesbian, Gay, Bisexual, Transgender, Queer, or Questioning *gaycenter.org*
7. Citizens with disabilities *ada.gov*
8. Survivors, Wounded, Censored, and Falsely Imprisoned
9. Immigrants
10. Individuals being the first… one of a few… or the last of…
11. _____

America's history, good and bad adjusts us to move better forward and laterally.
1. Legal, Human, and Voting rights violations
2. War & Suffrage
3. Hate, Racism, and Inequality
4. Losing & Winning
5. Abuse, Addiction, Intervention, Incarceration, Hospitalization, or unnecessary Death
6. Separation, Segregation, and Jim Crow
7. Injustice & Justice
8. Migration/Citizenship
9. Hunger, Poverty, and Pain
10. Incident/Accident
11. Love, Human kindness, Family & Friendship
12. Mother Nature's Violence, Destruction, or cause to Unite
13. _____

PLEASE CONTINUE TO SHARE YOU AND YOUR EXPERIENCES
Always share with others. Knowledge serves no purpose if not shared. How advantageous would it have been to you if someone had shared with you some need to know beforehand?

Driving through life, while being mindful that

Woke-up _____ on ____/_____/_____ M T W T F S S Hours of sleep ____

Sunny__ Cloudy__ Rainy__ Stormy__ Lightning__ Windy__ WTHail__ Snow__ WTMother Nature__

TODAY, I AM

☐	☐	☐	☐	☐	☐	STOP	☐	☐	☐	☐	☐	☐
GREAT	HOPEFUL	AWESOME	MINDFUL	BOLD	ENCOURAGED		GROUCHY	HURT	ANGRY	MAD	BELLIGERENT	ENRAGED
GOOD	HAPPY	ACTIVE	MOTIVATED	BRILLIANT	ENERGIZED		GUARDED	HATEFUL	ANNOYED	MOODY	BITTER	EXHAUSTED

TODAY, I AM GRATEFUL & EXCITED ABOUT:

_____

_____

_____

_____

_____

_____

LAST WORD IN ("Best Moment of Today" – "My Final Thought on Today" – "NOPE!, Never Again"):

$h!+ happeneds

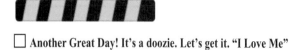

☐ **Another Great Day! It's a doozie. Let's get it. "I Love Me"**

Driving

> Some passengers will be okay with taking an around the way local drive but not anything longer.

through life

> Some people will be okay dating and hanging out but have no interest in a committed relationship.

while being mindful

> Every day isn't paradise. Everything is great until it's not. Never be secretive about anyone new in your life, especially when you're learning and evaluating if they should be a part of your personal space and life. If not family, someone close should always know the date, time, and location of your interaction with anyone new and unknown in case something goes wrong?

Some days -minus Some people equals= Some time for you. Take it and enjoy "Me Time".
A day in life is like driving down the road while eating your favorite box of chocolate. You can reach over, grab, and enjoy much as you want but soon as one piece of chocolate melts, crumbles, or breaks off; chocolate is smeared all over your clothes and the vehicle's interior is a mess.

Woke-up _____ on _____/_____/_____   M T W T F S S   Hours of sleep _____

Sunny__ Cloudy__ Rainy__ Stormy__ Lightning__ Windy__ WTHail__ Snow__ WTMother Nature__

TODAY, I AM

☐	☐	☐	☐	☐	☐	STOP	☐	☐	☐	☐	☐	☐
GREAT	HOPEFUL	AWESOME	MINDFUL	BOLD	ENCOURAGED		GROUCHY	HURT	ANGRY	MAD	BELLIGERENT	ENRAGED
GOOD	HAPPY	ACTIVE	MOTIVATED	BRILLIANT	ENERGIZED		GUARDED	HATEFUL	ANNOYED	MOODY	BITTER	EXHAUSTED

TODAY, I AM GRATEFUL & EXCITED ABOUT:

_____

_____

_____

_____

_____

_____

_____

_____

_____

_____

_____

_____

_____

_____

_____

_____

_____

_____

_____

_____

_____

_____

_____

_____

LAST WORD IN ("Best Moment of Today" – "My Final Thought on Today" – "NOPE!, Never Again"):

$h!+ happeneds

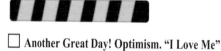

☐ **Another Great Day! Optimism. "I Love Me"**

Driving

> Never allow yourself to get upset or enraged over a parking stall you don't lease or own and probably never will park in it again.

through life

> Never allow yourself to get upset, enraged, or feel less of yourself if someone you like or admire doesn't feel the same about you.

while being mindful

Don't let your rage or anyone's rage toward you invalidate, institutionalize, incapacitate, or incarcerate a life being. Please make a note to seek help or assist other with anger issues and abusiveness (abuser & abused) before the anger and rage destroy a life.

Hospital, Morgues, Police/EMS Transport Vehicle, Locked/Hiding Room, Court Rooms, Confinement Center/Jail, Federal Prison, or Funeral Home

None of the above locations are the best place to admit, commit, promise, accept, or plead that you need help, anger management, professional assistance, intervention, safer reality, or better for yourself and others in harm's way. Before anger evolves to any above locations; please choose to help before it's a must have ("I should have" or "I wish I had…").

BE MINDFUL OF RAGE (extreme and violent):

RAGE (result of anger). Theres no do overs after rage is revealed. There's no way to forget visible or experienced rage. There's no love involved in rage. There's not guaranteed result after rage. Rage is unpredictable and unimaginable. Every act of rage involving physicality cause damage mentally. There's no one to blame for rage except the person enraged and out of control of themself. Rage in proportionally, in a higher degree, destroys and ends relationships and lives. There's no control if enraged. Rage is intense and dangerous. Rage always results in someone being frightened, hurt, or pained. Rage kills and change lives.

A type of rage: Road Rage

Woke-up _____ on _____/_____/_____   M T W T F S S   Hours of sleep _____

Sunny__ Cloudy__ Rainy__ Stormy__ Lightning__ Windy__ WTHail__ Snow__ WTMother Nature__

TODAY, I AM

☐	☐	☐	☐	☐	☐	STOP	☐	☐	☐	☐	☐	☐
GREAT	HOPEFUL	AWESOME	MINDFUL	BOLD	ENCOURAGED		GROUCHY	HURT	ANGRY	MAD	BELLIGERENT	ENRAGED
GOOD	HAPPY	ACTIVE	MOTIVATED	BRILLIANT	ENERGIZED		GUARDED	HATEFUL	ANNOYED	MOODY	BITTER	EXHAUSTED

TODAY, I AM GRATEFUL & EXCITED ABOUT:

_____

_____

_____

_____

_____

_____

_____

_____

_____

_____

_____

_____

_____

_____

_____

_____

_____

_____

_____

_____

_____

_____

_____

_____

_____

LAST WORD IN ("Best Moment of Today" – "My Final Thought on Today" – "NOPE!, Never Again"):

$h!+ happeneds

☐ **Another Great Day! It's celestial. "I Love Me"**

Driving

> Know your vehicle seating capacity (seatbelt)? How many passengers are required in a vehicle for a vehicle to operate safely?

through life

> How many people do you need in your inner circle to live your life?

while being mindful

> Anything you say out loud is for anyone who is listening. Anything you do is for anyone who is watching. If something personal and embarrassing happens in your life and is leaked and broadcasted to the public, would you know who talked?

Keep in mind to be mindful of who's being mindful of you.

1. Onlookers and those in earshot always talk.
2. News and online media influencers love talkers and graciously share their talk s.
3. Associate(s) and co-worker(s) always talk about you.
4. Some of your friends will talk with others they consider a closer friend.
5. Most individuals in a relationship talk with whom they're in relations.
6. Family talks and can't be trusted not to talk. You know those who have always been known to blab.
7. Some people talk about you to make themselves seem informed and better than you.
8. Some people talk about others to disguise and distract others from what's happening or going astray in their life.
9. Unless you easily leak your autobiography under the influence of special juices, you should know whom to trust with your most trusted info.
10. You have the right to remain silent and be still around individuals you don't know or trust because everything you say or do will be used against you in society's court.
11. It's more comforting to know who's around, listening, and sharing with you or of you.

Woke-up _____ on _____/_____/_____   M T W T F S S   Hours of sleep ____

Sunny__ Cloudy__ Rainy__ Stormy__   Lightning__ Windy__ WTHail__ Snow__ WTMother Nature__

TODAY, I AM

☐	☐	☐	☐	☐	☐	STOP	☐	☐	☐	☐	☐	☐
GREAT	HOPEFUL	AWESOME	MINDFUL	BOLD	ENCOURAGED		GROUCHY	HURT	ANGRY	MAD	BELLIGERENT	ENRAGED
GOOD	HAPPY	ACTIVE	MOTIVATED	BRILLIANT	ENERGIZED		GUARDED	HATEFUL	ANNOYED	MOODY	BITTER	EXHAUSTED

TODAY, I AM GRATEFUL & EXCITED ABOUT:

_____

_____

_____

_____

_____

_____

_____

_____

_____

_____

_____

_____

_____

_____

_____

_____

_____

_____

_____

_____

_____

_____

_____

_____

LAST WORD IN ("Best Moment of Today" – "My Final Thought on Today" – "NOPE!, Never Again"):

$h!+ happeneds

☐ **Another Great Day! I got that feeling. "I Love Me"**

Driving

If a vehicle you purchased had been manufactured and sold by a dealership with known unsafe defects, would you be loud and forthcoming about their cover-up or remain quiet and move on?

through life

Would you be loud and forthright if the history you were raised to believe was manufactured to cultivate a separate and biased system and further sold and financed by racist influencers, executives, leaders, and politicians for their purposeful racist agenda, or would you be quiet and dribble.

while being mindful

- Be cautious when seeing and hearing historical or privileged nonsense regurgitated because it can be upsetting and cause you to regurgitate with the same similarity.
- I don't eat meat or tolerate milk well, but I love my burgers with bacon and extra cheese.
- I can't entirely agree with freed enslaved families receiving 40 acres and mule, but I should be paid reparations for losing my right to transport, sell, trade illegally, and enslave them. (Broken Promise #15)
- I don't agree with or care for individuals having a homosexual relationship, but no one has the right to judge me for what I do sexually in my home/bed.
- I'm afraid I must disagree with women having the right to do whatever they want with their bodies, but no one woman can force me to have a vasectomy before having sexual relations.

Hypothesis or Hypocrisy:
I don't know why you're not understanding God and religion when I'm telling you about
1. My/Our God
2. My/Our beliefs
3. My/Our church
4. My/Our preacher's interpretations of the words
5. My/Our bible studies
6. My/Our understanding
7. My/Our supremacy or anointment of being favored
8. My/Our economics' status
9. My/Our patriotism
10. My/Our family history
11. My/Our privileges
12. My/Our education
13. My/Our interpretation
14. My/Our child's future
15. My/Our rights over your rights.
16. My/Our child's harm if they're educated as blacks' children were education as being slaves and imported but never as important to America's freedom and development.

Driving through life, while being mindful that

Woke-up _____ on ____/____/_____ M T W T F S S Hours of sleep ____

Sunny__ Cloudy__ Rainy__ Stormy__ Lightning__ Windy__ WTHail__ Snow__ WTMother Nature__

TODAY, I AM

☐	☐	☐	☐	☐	☐	**STOP**	☐	☐	☐	☐	☐	☐
GREAT	HOPEFUL	AWESOME	MINDFUL	BOLD	ENCOURAGED		GROUCHY	HURT	ANGRY	MAD	BELLIGERENT	ENRAGED
GOOD	HAPPY	ACTIVE	MOTIVATED	BRILLIANT	ENERGIZED		GUARDED	HATEFUL	ANNOYED	MOODY	BITTER	EXHAUSTED

TODAY, I AM GRATEFUL & EXCITED ABOUT:

_____

_____

_____

_____

_____

_____

_____

_____

_____

_____

_____

_____

_____

_____

_____

_____

_____

_____

_____

_____

_____

_____

_____

_____

_____

_____

LAST WORD IN ("Best Moment of Today" – "My Final Thought on Today" – "NOPE!, Never Again"):

$h!+ happeneds

☐ **Another Great Day! Achieved. Get out of my way! "I Love Me"**

Conscious or Confusions?

1. Do you think people should be outraged about wild and free animals being hunted, put in cages, forced to breed, and displayed in zoos, circuses, or exhibits for adult amusement/funds?

2. Do you think a race of people wrongly hunted, kidnapped, caged, tortured, beaten, separated, raped, stripped of lineage, forced to breed, put on display for auction, condemned, given less than animals or equal to and in some known injustice cases even to be lynched, burned, and shot to death should remain fated or still be feeling some way?

3. If you were wrongly imprisoned' would you expect to receive automatic reparations? If your child suffered mentally, socially, or financially while you were wrongly imprisoned, would you expect your children to be feeling some way?

4. Do you think a person wrongly imprisoned should remain incarcerated and afforded no less than an apology with their citizen's rights re-instated?

5. Do you think a person's history of social media posts, legal incidents, citations, arrests, or convictions should be used against them?

6. Do you think a public service leader or police officer with a racist history should be given a pass?

7. Should farmers receive government debt relief assistance or loans?

8. Should farmers of a different shade of color be able to receive government debt relief assistance or loans?

9. Do you think a race of people legally imprisoned by unjust laws, demoralized by systematic racism, and whose ancestry has been WHAAATE Washed should settle and be thankful for being in a room but not at the table unless servicing, building, or standby until needed?

10. Do you think a race of people marginalized, economically wronged, and unfavorably treated for employment, loans, education (G.I Bill failure), land and property ownership, and rights to vote receive repairation and reparations?

11. Should a race of descendants remain passive, quiet, and content about their ancestors being forced onto slavery plantations, government reservations, and unjust medical projects? Should they not be outraged and outspoken about slave plantation owners' descendants inheriting or reaping the head start and rewards in economics, education, historical publications, and the American Dream?

"A man is a man, until that man finds a plan, a plan that makes that man, a new man." Dred Scott

Woke-up _____ on ____/_____/_____ M T W T F S S   Hours of sleep ____

Sunny__ Cloudy__ Rainy__ Stormy__ Lightning__ Windy__ WTHail__ Snow__ WTMother Nature__

TODAY, I AM

☐ ☐ ☐ ☐ ☐ ☐ **STOP** ☐ ☐ ☐ ☐ ☐ ☐

| GREAT | HOPEFUL | AWESOME | MINDFUL | BOLD | ENCOURAGED | GROUCHY | HURT | ANGRY | MAD | BELLIGERENT | ENRAGED |
| GOOD | HAPPY | ACTIVE | MOTIVATED | BRILLIANT | ENERGIZED | GUARDED | HATEFUL | ANNOYED | MOODY | BITTER | EXHAUSTED |

TODAY, I AM GRATEFUL & EXCITED ABOUT:

_____

_____
_____
_____
_____
_____
_____
_____
_____
_____
_____
_____
_____
_____
_____
_____
_____
_____
_____
_____
_____
_____
_____
_____
_____
_____

LAST WORD IN ("Best Moment of Today" – "My Final Thought on Today" – "NOPE!, Never Again"):

_____

$h!+ happeneds

☐ **BAM! Another Great Day! "I Love Me"**

WHO ARE YOU? ARE YOU, BECAUSE OF YOU? IS YOUR LIFE BECAUSE OF YOU?
An only if scenario: A citizen's wishful correspondence with a uniformed police officer who has requested a citizen to identify themselves without the officer having any reasonable suspicion, probable crime, law violation, complainant, or criminal act in performance to solicit identification:

Police- "I need to see your ID."
Citizen- Who are you?
Uniformed Officer- I'm Police Officer _____.
Citizen- Who are you?
Police- Police Officer _____.
Citizen- WHO ARE YOU?
Police- Again, I'M OFFICER _____ BADGE# _____.
Citizen- Again, OFFICER. WHO ARE YOU?
Police- silence
Citizen- Citizen Peace Officer _____ Badge# _____ Who are you?
Citizen- Citizen Peace Officer _____ Badge# _____ Who-Are-YOU?
Police- cricket-cricket-cricket (facial frustration)
Citizen- Who am I? (facial relaxation)
I am a citizen
I'm a citizen just like you, Peace Officer _____.
I'm a citizen like your family member, Peach Officer _____.
I'm a citizen. The same citizen as you out of uniform if an officer of another jurisdiction was violating your rights.
I'm a citizen frustrated with dealing with police officers, police stations, police departments, resignation/rehiring, police associations, and unions protecting the bad apples and viruses infecting and corrupting the good and needed PEACE OFFFICERS.
I'm a citizen who prefers PEACE OFFICERS who are citizens within the community they serve.
I'm a citizen who prefers PEACE OFFICERS that mirror their communities' diversity.
I'm a citizen who needs PEACE OFFICERS. I am aware of that. Are you aware that I am aware PEACE OFFICER _____?
I'm a citizen who needs PEACE OFFICERS who didn't take an oath to protect and serve the blue line over their community and their citizen's rights.
I'm a citizen who needs the PEACE OFFICERS who swore an oath of being peace officers, being the peace, seeking peace, de-escalating for peace, keeping the peace, and sustaining the peace.
I'm a citizen who needs PEACE OFFICERS who hold **all**, including fellow bad officers, accountable for not making their peace toward one another by law, humanity, and citizen's rights.
Lastly, I'm a citizen who should be afforded my constitutional rights when stopped, questioned, detained, or arrested by a peace officer. The rights that protect each citizen from any law enforcement officer's unsolicited, unwarranted, biased, personal indifferences, and unprofessional interaction or illegitimacy.
Citizen- Officer. Who are you? Are you a PEACE OFFICER? Are you the officer we need for our community to thrive in peace instead of fear, bias, chaos, or supremacy idiocy and ideology?
If you are. NICE TO MEET YOU PEACE OFFICER _____.

Woke-up _____ on ____/____/____   M T W T F S S   Hours of sleep ____

Sunny__ Cloudy__ Rainy__ Stormy__ Lightning__ Windy__ WTHail__ Snow__ WTMother Nature__

TODAY, I AM

☐	☐	☐	☐	☐	☐	🛑	☐	☐	☐	☐	☐	☐
GREAT	HOPEFUL	AWESOME	MINDFUL	BOLD	ENCOURAGED		GROUCHY	HURT	ANGRY	MAD	BELLIGERENT	ENRAGED
GOOD	HAPPY	ACTIVE	MOTIVATED	BRILLIANT	ENERGIZED		GUARDED	HATEFUL	ANNOYED	MOODY	BITTER	EXHAUSTED

TODAY, I AM GRATEFUL & EXCITED ABOUT:

_____

_____

_____

_____

_____

_____

_____

_____

_____

_____

_____

_____

_____

_____

_____

_____

_____

_____

_____

_____

_____

_____

_____

_____

_____

LAST WORD IN ("Best Moment of Today" – "My Final Thought on Today" – "NOPE!, Never Again"):

$h!+ happeneds

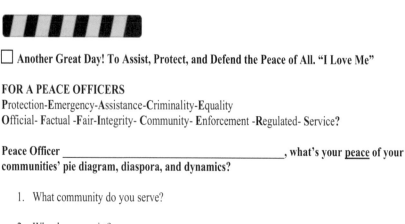

☐ **Another Great Day! To Assist, Protect, and Defend the Peace of All. "I Love Me"**

FOR A PEACE OFFICERS
Protection-Emergency-Assistance-Criminality-Equality
Official- Factual -Fair-Integrity- Community- Enforcement -Regulated- Service?

Peace Officer _____, what's your <u>peace</u> of your communities' pie diagram, diaspora, and dynamics?

1. What community do you serve?

2. Who do you assist?

3. Who do you protect?

4. Who do you defend?

5. Do you treat every emergency the same?

6. Is every person a criminal until proven guilty or innocent until you've proven who's involved, or with an association?

7. Are you involved (living, dining, or shopping) in the community you serve?

8. What are you doing in the community you serve other than policing?

9. Are you performing your official duties as a sworn officer?

10. Are you operating by law and facts or by another's personal bias, beliefs, or hearsay?

11. Are you treating every citizen with guilt immediately or by the words of another without any area canvassing, corroborating, or investigating?

12. Are your procedures regulated and enforced by your training, fellow officers, or leaders?

13. Do you have integrity, or do you go along with another's bad or others in blue w/o thought?

14. Should a citizen feel safe, cautious, or fearful in your present?

15. Are you fair and equal to every citizen and are their rights the same?

16. Are citizens being treated as you would hope your loved family members is treated?

No discord, dislike, or disrespect. I hope Safety and Peace Be Unto All Officers. Thank you

Driving through life, while being mindful that

0001 ANOTHER ONE!

FT GHAMBE

Woke-up _____ on ____/____/____ M T W T F S S   Hours of sleep ____

Sunny_ Cloudy_ Rainy_ Stormy_ Lightning_ Windy_ WTHail_ Snow_ WTMother Nature_

TODAY, I AM

☐	☐	☐	☐	☐	☐	STOP	☐	☐	☐	☐	☐	☐
GREAT	HOPEFUL	AWESOME	MINDFUL	BOLD	ENCOURAGED		GROUCHY	HURT	ANGRY	MAD	BELLIGERENT	ENRAGED
GOOD	HAPPY	ACTIVE	MOTIVATED	BRILLIANT	ENERGIZED		GUARDED	HATEFUL	ANNOYED	MOODY	BITTER	EXHAUSTED

TODAY, I AM GRATEFUL & EXCITED ABOUT:

_____

_____

_____

_____

_____

_____

_____

_____

_____

_____

_____

_____

_____

_____

_____

_____

_____

_____

_____

_____

_____

_____

LAST WORD IN ("Best Moment of Today" – "My Final Thought on Today" – "NOPE!, Never Again"):

_____

$h!+ happeneds

☐ **Another Great Day! Again, encouraging. "I Love Me"**

Driving

Your hate for your first vehicle can lead you to dislike the next vehicle of the same make or model and limit your selection in the future. No vehicle is perfect, and no drive is perfect.

through life

One unpleasant experience with a person in a group or organization shouldn't make all within that group terrible. There's no such thing as meeting the perfect person or having a perfect life, and nobody is immune from hateful looks, words, or bias.

while being mindful
What ifs….
1. No vehicle breaks down or requires mechanical repair. Would the parts manufacturing industry, dealerships, and world trade suffer?
2. No parties or events were held for birthdays, elementary move up, middle school culminations, proms, high school graduation, tech/college graduation, anniversaries, or whatever recognition day. Would the local economies suffer?
3. Everybody was a genius. Would our conversations, attraction, or educational system suffer?
4. Everybody lives forever. Would our food, water supply, and utility services suffer?
5. Everybody had love in their heart and mind. Would our military, politics, news media, and legal system be or suffer?
6. Everybody lives a healthier lifestyle. Would the medical and pharmaceutical conglomerates be or suffer?
7. Everybody was humane. Would racism, competition, separatism, elitism, hatred, and animosity amongst one another exist?
8. Everybody was allowed to practice or be within their chosen faith, worship, religion, spirituality, or not. Would racism, competition, elitism, separatism, jealousy, inequalities, and animosity amongst religions exist?
9. Everybody was treated equally and humanely. Would the prison system, gov't hidden earmarks, and most politicians' careers be, and would their fear-mongering and divisive politics for donations suffer?
10. Everybody agreed about better gun control measures in the future. Would the medical, law enforcement, and legal careers suffer, and the penal system continues to expand?
11. Everybody was wealthy. Would customer servicing, construction, security infrastructure, farming, manufacturing, maintenance, public service, military, government, or labor be or suffer?
12. Every adult didn't have a childhood focus on receiving Christmas toys. Would our economy suffer at the end of the year?
13. Everybody didn't eat three times a day as indoctrinated when to eat (Breakfast/ Lunch//Dinner). Would our economy suffer? Would adults be healthier and smaller?
14. Every adult didn't grow on sugary products as a child. Would our health be better?
15. We celebrate our children's careers or first apartment or home instead of educational graduations. Would our children suffer or look forward to their ultimate celebration?

Driving through life, while being mindful that

Woke-up _____ on ____/____/____   M T W T F S S   Hours of sleep ____

Sunny__ Cloudy__ Rainy__ Stormy__ Lightning__ Windy__ WTHail__ Snow__ WTMother Nature__

TODAY, I AM

☐	☐	☐	☐	☐	☐	STOP	☐	☐	☐	☐	☐	☐
GREAT	HOPEFUL	AWESOME	MINDFUL	BOLD	ENCOURAGED		GROUCHY	HURT	ANGRY	MAD	BELLIGERENT	ENRAGED
GOOD	HAPPY	ACTIVE	MOTIVATED	BRILLIANT	ENERGIZED		GUARDED	HATEFUL	ANNOYED	MOODY	BITTER	EXHAUSTED

TODAY, I AM GRATEFUL & EXCITED ABOUT:

_____

_____

_____

_____

_____

_____

_____

_____

_____

_____

_____

_____

_____

_____

_____

_____

_____

_____

_____

_____

_____

_____

_____

_____

LAST WORD IN ("Best Moment of Today" – "My Final Thought on Today" – "NOPE!, Never Again"):

$h!+ happeneds

☐ **Another Great Day! I'm needed some way, somehow, or somewhere. "I Love Me"**

Driving
> Bad driving can cost you everything. Nobody wants to ride with a bad driver.

Life
> Bad living can cost you everything. Nobody wants to be around bad all the time.

while being mindful
> Accessing the internet is like opening the door of your room or home and leaving it open. Be careful who you allow into your mind and spirit.

Checkout: Internet Safety Links

Internet Safety 101 –
https://internetsafety101.org

CISA.gov –
https://www.cisa.gov/cyber-safety

Consumer Federal Trade Commission –
https://consumer.ftc.gov/identity-theft-and-online-security/online-privacy-and-security

Kids Safe learning –
https://sos.fbi.gov/en/

National Elder Fraud Hotline 1-833-FRAUD-11 (1-833-372-8311) -
https://ovc.ojp.gov/program/stop-elder-fraud/providing-help-restoring-hope

IC3.gov –
https://www.ic3.gov/
The IC3 accepts online Internet crime complaints from either the actual victim or from a third party to the complainant.

Disclaimer:
The included links, along with content contained therein do not constitute an endorsement by FT GHAMBE. The sites are used solely for information. FT GHAMBE does not exercise any editorial control over the information you may find at these sites.

Driving through life, while being mindful that

Woke-up _____ on ____/____/____   M T W T F S S   Hours of sleep ____

Sunny__ Cloudy__ Rainy__ Stormy__   Lightning__ Windy__ WTHail__ Snow__ WTMother Nature__

TODAY, I AM

☐	☐	☐	☐	☐	☐	STOP	☐	☐	☐	☐	☐	☐
GREAT	HOPEFUL	AWESOME	MINDFUL	BOLD	ENCOURAGED		GROUCHY	HURT	ANGRY	MAD	BELLIGERENT	ENRAGED
GOOD	HAPPY	ACTIVE	MOTIVATED	BRILLIANT	ENERGIZED		GUARDED	HATEFUL	ANNOYED	MOODY	BITTER	EXHAUSTED

TODAY, I AM GRATEFUL & EXCITED ABOUT:

_____
_____
_____
_____
_____
_____
_____
_____
_____
_____
_____
_____
_____
_____
_____
_____
_____
_____
_____
_____
_____
_____
_____
_____

LAST WORD IN ("Best Moment of Today" – "My Final Thought on Today" – "NOPE!, Never Again"):

$h!+ happeneds

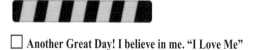

☐ **Another Great Day! I believe in me. "I Love Me"**

Driving
What additives and chemicals are included in your vehicle's lubricant and fluids? Are they safe for the life use of my vehicle?

through life
What's in vaccines? What's in every product you consume in your body?

while being mindful
- Do you plant, grow, or make everything you eat?
- Do you know the ingredients of everything you eat or drink?
- Do you believe ingredient labels are designed for you or other vital disapprovals regarding consumable products and their labeling?
- So many people find themselves politically and specifically motivated about one Financially Dangerous Association's COVID vaccine approval but no concern about past Funded Dangerous Associations' approvals. Another history lesson in why manufacturing lobbyists and business elites thrived then and now and why product labels are for marketing and selling to consumers; not protecting:

Currently displayed on product labels.
1. No Farce Dangerous Association, or agency regulates vitamins and dietary supplements.
2. Naturally & Artificially Flavored
3. No sugar added: sweet/other natural flavor but zero added sugar?
4. No sugar but sweetened with_____ sweetener.
5. No sugar but ingredient words ending with "ose" means apparent sugar exchange (cheap).
6. You see 180 Calories (fine print--5 servings per person)
7. If your reading label is small or barely readable, there's some unknown being glossed over.
8. Reference ingredients "Statements evaluated by "Fearful Dangerous Association." but not the product.
9. Made in a Financially Dangerous Area registered place.
10. Reference ingredients "This statement has not been evaluated."
11. Imported, Manufactured, Packaged, Processed, and Distributed from where?
12. We never test on animals (who/what tested on?)
13. What are Inactive ingredients vs. Active ingredients?
14. Made in the USA but imported?
15. Plant-based (If a plant is a base, what's on top of that base?)
16. Not for retail sale-Pharmacy dispensary only means higher cost.
17. Certified Vegan, Certified Gluten Free, Certified Organic, GMO (who certifies the certifiers, which regulated who, who sanctioned who, who donated to who, and who financed who?)

***Everything labeled vegan (highly/ultra-processed) isn't healthy, and many types of foods and beverages marketed as not having any sugar (no sugar, 0% sugar) have a sugar substitute or sweetener (manufactured sweetness or fakeness).

Driving through life, while being mindful that

Woke-up _____ on ____/_____/_____ M T W T F S S Hours of sleep ____

Sunny__ Cloudy__ Rainy__ Stormy__ Lightning__ Windy__ WTHail__ Snow__ WTMother Nature__

TODAY, I AM

☐ ☐ ☐ ☐ ☐ ☐ **STOP** ☐ ☐ ☐ ☐ ☐ ☐

| GREAT | HOPEFUL | AWESOME | MINDFUL | BOLD | ENCOURAGED | | GROUCHY | HURT | ANGRY | MAD | BELLIGERENT | ENRAGED |
| GOOD | HAPPY | ACTIVE | MOTIVATED | BRILLIANT | ENERGIZED | | GUARDED | HATEFUL | ANNOYED | MOODY | BITTER | EXHAUSTED |

TODAY, I AM GRATEFUL & EXCITED ABOUT:

_____

_____
_____
_____
_____
_____
_____
_____
_____
_____
_____
_____
_____
_____
_____
_____
_____
_____
_____
_____
_____
_____
_____
_____
_____

LAST WORD IN ("Best Moment of Today" – "My Final Thought on Today" – "NOPE!, Never Again"):

$h!+ happeneds

☐ **Another Great Day! It's time to tap in. "I Love Me"**

1. Are secret recipe ingredients known of and approved by the FDA?

2. Who checks and balances the World Health Organization?

3. Is Better Business Bureau a better business? Who regulates BBB?

4. How good is a charity if its funds' transparency is hidden/private?

5. Why aren't tax exempted records publicly available?

6. What outside agency checks on state lotteries, especially with anonymous winners?

7. Do philanthropies shield billions or trillions from taxes?

8. Is creating a tax-exempt religious, political, or charitable organization easier or harder than vaccine exemptions?

9. Why isn't there an online transparency list for the taxpayer to view down to the cent for every fund allocated to a state awarded a contract with the reasoning behind a company being awarded or not awarded?

10. Where are the financial schematics for every state government or federal-funded fund infrastructure contract available down to every dollar distributed?

11. How many appreciative large political donors are awarded or reciprocated with thank you contracts?

12. What percentage of a politician's statement "Let me be clear" alludes to suspicion, falsehood, reflection, misdirection, or a red flag?

13. Why do we legitimize partial, or part of products as "American Made" but not people? An individual born in FT GHAMBE, GA but grouped as African American. Why are we still racing one another? Is there still a winner and loser in a race? Is the race winner consistently awarded or afforded something more? Who are the owners of the racetracks? Can a race be fixed, or another given an advantage? Who's tired of racing? Why do we have to race every day? Why are we forcing children and our children's children to continue to pursue this dangerous form of racing that still results in injuries and deaths?

14. What does ROI mean to you?
    - ☐ Return on Investment
    - ☐ The righteousness of Investors/Investee?
    - ☐ Release of Information Act
    - ☐ Rights of Institutions? (a department's right to block, delay, or limit what's released)
    - ☐ Risk of Infection
    - ☐ Racism Obviously Involved

Driving through life, while being mindful that

Woke-up _____ on ____/____/_____   M T W T F S S   Hours of sleep ____

Sunny_   Cloudy_   Rainy_   Stormy_   Lightning_   Windy_   WTHail_   Snow_ WTMother Nature_

TODAY, I AM

☐ GREAT / GOOD   ☐ HOPEFUL / HAPPY   ☐ AWESOME / ACTIVE   ☐ MINDFUL / MOTIVATED   ☐ BOLD / BRILLIANT   ☐ ENCOURAGED / ENERGIZED   **STOP**   ☐ GROUCHY / GUARDED   ☐ HURT / HATEFUL   ☐ ANGRY / ANNOYED   ☐ MAD / MOODY   ☐ BELLIGERENT / BITTER   ☐ ENRAGED / EXHAUSTED

TODAY, I AM GRATEFUL & EXCITED ABOUT:

_____

_____

_____

_____

_____

_____

_____

_____

_____

_____

_____

_____

_____

_____

_____

_____

_____

_____

_____

_____

_____

_____

_____

LAST WORD IN ("Best Moment of Today" – "My Final Thought on Today" – "NOPE!, Never Again"):

$h!+ happeneds

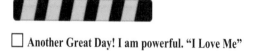

☐ **Another Great Day! I am powerful. "I Love Me"**

Driving

It doesn't matter if your engine is running; never leave a child or pet in an unattended vehicle. A child or pet can't and won't take care of themselves. What happens if no one knows of a running vehicle that stops running and overheats?

through life

What happens if there is an incident or emergency in the place you momentarily walked in for service, and no one knows of your helpless keiki, kupuna, pipi'i, ohana, or a healthcare-immobile person who is unattended in a vehicle or home alone in your care responsibility?

while being mindful

Never leave an unattended child, senior, pet, or someone dependent on your care alone without anyone's knowledge and assistance:

1. What happens if you become unavailable, unconscious, or medically incapacitated, and someone is awaiting your return and responsible care?
2. What contingency plan do you have in place for a living species in your care if you don't return for some unsuspecting reason or timeframe?
3. What happens if no one knows of the running vehicle and the vehicle stops running and overheats?
4. Who in the building knows of a child or pet in the vehicle alone? Unconscious YOU
5. Who in the building knows of a child or pet in the vehicle alone and in dire need of water, cold/cool air, food, and emergency medical assistance? Incoherent or Selfish YOU

Woke-up _____ on ____/____/_____   M T W T F S S   Hours of sleep ____

Sunny__ Cloudy__ Rainy__ Stormy__ Lightning__ Windy__ WTHail__ Snow__ WTMother Nature__

TODAY, I AM

☐ ☐ ☐ ☐ ☐ ☐ **STOP** ☐ ☐ ☐ ☐ ☐ ☐

| GREAT | HOPEFUL | AWESOME | MINDFUL | BOLD | ENCOURAGED | | GROUCHY | HURT | ANGRY | MAD | BELLIGERENT | ENRAGED |
| GOOD | HAPPY | ACTIVE | MOTIVATED | BRILLIANT | ENERGIZED | | GUARDED | HATEFUL | ANNOYED | MOODY | BITTER | EXHAUSTED |

TODAY, I AM GRATEFUL & EXCITED ABOUT:

_____

_____

_____

_____

_____

_____

_____

_____

_____

_____

_____

_____

_____

_____

_____

_____

_____

_____

_____

_____

_____

_____

_____

LAST WORD IN ("Best Moment of Today" – "My Final Thought on Today" – "NOPE!, Never Again"):

$h!+ happeneds

☐ **Another Great Day! Something to talk about in the break room. "I Love Me"**

Driving

Ride or Die (Yielding Right-of-Way) You pull up to the intersection to turn left, but the vehicle in the adjacent front lane has the right of way to proceed first. The light turns green, but the other car hesitates. Should you wait or proceed? Are there any other drivers affected?

through life

Knowing when to seize the moments or not too. Some people are hesitant in all they do, and deciding if you should wait on them, make the first move, or move on can be difficult and exhausting. The time you pause your life waiting for someone to do, do right, or finally do what is needed or required is time you'll never get back and be reimbursed. We are all here for a limited time, and you must be sure someone deserves your precious time.

while being mindful

Invaluable time is time wasted and shared with someone who doesn't value you or your time. Most individuals give most of their time to individuals whom they have no relations with or can reciprocate some time back in return (artists, actors, entertainers, celebrities, athletes, influencers, Karen like individuals, politicians, tobacco and alcohol beverage makers, or relations sucking your lifetime away). If you are giving someone your time, please make sure it's time being enjoyed by you as well; it not Free Up Calendar, Keep Every Minute.

Justifiable use of time estimate: =righteous time to be more, do more, or share more.

672 hours a month to be grateful and appreciative.
minus 160hrs to work, educational, internship, or volunteer week.
minus 40hrs of work prep and travel time
minus 72hrs of self-growth mentally/physically/spiritually).

=400 hours of self (eat/sleep), family, friends, socializing, and additional self-growth

Unjustifiable use of time estimate: =no time to be more, do more, or share more.

672 hours a month to be appreciating.
minus 336hrs of hurting others and doing wrong (robbing, assaulting, illegally acquiring whatever, soliciting, scamming, drug mule, and pawning self and items for trade, or hospitalization
minus 280hrs dope fiending (searching, abusing, sleep deprivation, incoherent, or being abused and taken advantage of).
minus 56hrs of rush, euphoria, paranoia, hallucination, incoherence, loss of memory loss, starvation, semi-unconscious, reflecting, anger, shame, aching, abuse, and fighting to live for another day.

=3 hours of family time or a chance at possible intervention

Driving through life, while being mindful that

Woke-up _____ on _____/_____/_____   M T W T F S S   Hours of sleep _____

Sunny__ Cloudy__ Rainy__ Stormy__ Lightning__ Windy__ WTHail__ Snow__ WTMother Nature__

TODAY, I AM

☐	☐	☐	☐	☐	☐	STOP	☐	☐	☐	☐	☐	☐
GREAT	HOPEFUL	AWESOME	MINDFUL	BOLD	ENCOURAGED		GROUCHY	HURT	ANGRY	MAD	BELLIGERENT	ENRAGED
GOOD	HAPPY	ACTIVE	MOTIVATED	BRILLIANT	ENERGIZED		GUARDED	HATEFUL	ANNOYED	MOODY	BITTER	EXHAUSTED

TODAY, I AM GRATEFUL & EXCITED ABOUT:

_____

_____
_____
_____
_____
_____
_____
_____
_____
_____
_____
_____
_____
_____
_____
_____
_____
_____
_____
_____
_____
_____
_____
_____

LAST WORD IN ("Best Moment of Today" – "My Final Thought on Today" – "NOPE!, Never Again"):

$h!+ happeneds

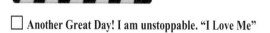

☐ **Another Great Day! I am unstoppable. "I Love Me"**

Driving
> Don't approach your vehicle if you see something odd and suspicious on or near your vehicle because it could be a trap or allow someone unsuspecting to be your savior as they planned.

through life
> Don't allow any person in your space of peace or life when their presence makes you feel suspicious, unsafe, or uncomforting.

while being mindful
> Why is everything illegal until the government enterprise and the politicians see the financial gains?
> 1. Illegal cocaine distribution to Opioid pharmaceutical prescription (political donations)
> 2. Illegal numbers/betting to State Lotteries
> 3. Alcohol prohibition to Legalize Alcohol
> 4. Marijuana illegal use/distribution/prison franchising to Legalize Marijuana ("Fixin to" be like purchasing your favorite alcoholic beverage on Sundays down south.)
> 5. Mafia protection vs. Government taxing/contracts
> 6. Loan Shark % vs. Bank & Credit Corporate fees and interest rates
> 7. Illegal trade vs. International trade agreements (cheap labor/low cost/product increases profit margin)
> 8. United Nations of trade agreements/quid pro quos/cheap labor
> 9. Too Much Government vs. Government savior programs and funding
> 10. Illegal overseas bank account to hide money vs. Government bills, contracts to win over senator holdout agreements without any money transparency
> 11. Illegal immigrants to Undocumented Cheap laborers for companies to keep cost down and profits churning. "**BUT** it because they use fake SSN and identification not because we didn't do our due diligence in vetting or verifying through E-Verify process."
> 12. Political donations vs. quid pro quo (guaranteed cabinet or board seat appointment, property purchase at less than market value, speaking engagements payment, book deal, associate/family member benefiting or being rewarded with a government contract.

Please, be cautious of a few
1. Be cautious of somebody that supposedly will look away of your wrong, illegal, or misstep today?
2. Be cautious of somebody with evidential knowledge of your misstep or crime today?
3. Be cautious of somebody doing a lifesaving <u>favor</u> for you today.
4. Be cautious of somebody is offering you an illegal way to make some extra cash today.
5. Be cautious of somebody eagerly offering you time or something of theirs today upon your arrival in an unfamiliar environment (dorm, jail, prison, group, or organization)? Something gracious of someone today could be a steep price tomorrow with a high-interest rate (favor) taxed on or with no return value in your future.

Driving through life, while being mindful that

Woke-up _____ on ____/____/____ M T W T F S S   Hours of sleep ____

Sunny__ Cloudy__ Rainy__ Stormy__ Lightning__ Windy__ WTHail__ Snow__ WTMother Nature__

TODAY, I AM

☐	☐	☐	☐	☐	☐	STOP	☐	☐	☐	☐	☐	☐
GREAT	HOPEFUL	AWESOME	MINDFUL	BOLD	ENCOURAGED		GROUCHY	HURT	ANGRY	MAD	BELLIGERENT	ENRAGED
GOOD	HAPPY	ACTIVE	MOTIVATED	BRILLIANT	ENERGIZED		GUARDED	HATEFUL	ANNOYED	MOODY	BITTER	EXHAUSTED

TODAY, I AM GRATEFUL & EXCITED ABOUT:

LAST WORD IN ("Best Moment of Today" – "My Final Thought on Today" – "NOPE!, Never Again"):

$h!+ happeneds

☐ Attention / Parade Rest / Stand at Ease / Rest. Another Great Day! "I Love Me"

"BREAKING NEWS!"

I interrupt your reading and journaling to bring you this special piece of peaceful information. Set your mood to "Energetic" or "Great day to be me" today and take a news radio and television news broadcasting day off. <u>Do Not</u> turn on or allow anyone's negative news-producing energy to bombard your day (drive in silence). If riding, ride in your silence (no electronics or phone) and listen to what's going on around you. The silence will assist you in visualizing more and possibly notice someone being missed and overlooked. **Now back to your regular schedule journaling.**

Woke-up _____ on ____/____/____ M T W T F S S   Hours of sleep ____

Sunny__ Cloudy__ Rainy__ Stormy__ Lightning__ Windy__ WTHail__ Snow__ WTMother Nature__

TODAY, I AM

☐	☐	☐	☐	☐	☐	STOP	☐	☐	☐	☐	☐	☐
GREAT	HOPEFUL	AWESOME	MINDFUL	BOLD	ENCOURAGED		GROUCHY	HURT	ANGRY	MAD	BELLIGERENT	ENRAGED
GOOD	HAPPY	ACTIVE	MOTIVATED	BRILLIANT	ENERGIZED		GUARDED	HATEFUL	ANNOYED	MOODY	BITTER	EXHAUSTED

TODAY, I AM GRATEFUL & EXCITED ABOUT:

_____

_____

_____

_____

_____

_____

_____

_____

_____

_____

_____

_____

_____

_____

_____

_____

_____

_____

_____

_____

_____

_____

_____

_____

_____

LAST WORD IN ("Best Moment of Today" – "My Final Thought on Today" – "NOPE!, Never Again"):

$h!+ happeneds

☐ **Another Great Day! Bask in its beauty. "I Love Me"**

Driving

Any vehicle lights left on will lead to a dead battery. Check the battery by jump starting or replacement if the vehicle dashboard and lights are dimming or clicking sound when turning the ignition when trying to jump . "Dead as a Doornail"

through life

Rest. Turn yourself off, or you will expire quicker than most. A few "tell-tale signs" you need to replace a few hours of your do time with rest time is when you're yarning, head nodding, and unknowingly staring at the inside of your eyelids when you're supposed to be awakened.

while being mindful

Rest is one of the secrets to a long life.

Your time is a hot commodity. "The hottest"

1. Share your time with your family. Have fun by creating a time coupon book to share minutes-hours coupons with a family member (minutes or hours equivalent to your age, their age, anniversary, particular date, or favorite number)
2. Have a "Me day" plan (Read or draft a chapter/short story/book, complete drawing/painting, scan old photos to digital, start a puzzle or add another puzzle piece, meditate, or seek 15min.-45min. of alone/quiet time, or listen/dance to favorite music)
3. Go back in reminiscence times and catch up with long time no see "my friend," "my buddy," "my fellow veteran," "my classmate," "my mentor," …
4. Say thank you or gift a thank you card or note to a parent, friend, bus driver, teacher, patient service member, first responder, hospitality representative, mentor, elder, employee, customer service provider, health professional, service member, or entertainer.
5. Talk and share some love, knowledge, history, or a joke with someone in person (real-time).
6. Go outside and enjoy the weather, traffic, nature's beauty, noises, and animals.
7. Connect with someone old, young, or feeling forgotten.
8. Go to a library, park, track/trail, or gym.
9. Go to your favorite or new restaurant to dine in or eat somewhere away from your residence.
10. Emphasis on a new day, new you, and new beginning.
11. Home time (try a recipe, cook a meal, clean, store items, yard sale or complete an overdue maintenance repair/project)
12. Plan or revisit a re-location idea, dream, or plan. Plan a vacation or weekend getaway.
13. Volunteer some of your time into positive service time to and for others.
14. Use your non-dominate hand as the dominant hand all day.
15. Take a social media, internet, AI, video gaming, or news/politics day off.
16. Stop stressing and doing way too much and going nowhere.
17. Go to your medical checkups to get all the required medical care and knowledge to live and thrive longer.

Driving through life, while being mindful that

Woke-up _____ on ____/____/_____   M T W T F S S   Hours of sleep ____

Sunny__ Cloudy__ Rainy__ Stormy__ Lightning__ Windy__ WTHail__ Snow__ WTMother Nature__

TODAY, I AM

☐	☐	☐	☐	☐	☐	STOP	☐	☐	☐	☐	☐	☐
GREAT	HOPEFUL	AWESOME	MINDFUL	BOLD	ENCOURAGED		GROUCHY	HURT	ANGRY	MAD	BELLIGERENT	ENRAGED
GOOD	HAPPY	ACTIVE	MOTIVATED	BRILLIANT	ENERGIZED		GUARDED	HATEFUL	ANNOYED	MOODY	BITTER	EXHAUSTED

TODAY, I AM GRATEFUL & EXCITED ABOUT:

_____

_____

_____

_____

_____

_____

_____

_____

_____

_____

_____

_____

_____

_____

_____

_____

_____

_____

_____

_____

_____

_____

_____

_____

_____

LAST WORD IN ("Best Moment of Today" – "My Final Thought on Today" – "NOPE!, Never Again"):

$h!+ happeneds

☐ **Another Great Day! Appreciative but caution is still necessary. "I Love Me"**

Driving

When teaching someone how to drive, be cautious that you don't allow your style of teaching (chastising) to come off as demeaning.

through life

Be careful of the past you continue to pass on. What you consider being or becoming an adult, woman, or man may be chastising and intimidating to others? What's laughed at and shrugged off by you can be humiliating and hurtful to someone else.

while being mindful

What made you, made you, but it didn't create a similar doppelganger. The same pressure that helped developed you may be crushing to another.

- You don't listen to another's point of view because it made you.
- You don't speak or show love because it made you.
- You don't hug because it made you.
- You don't discourage mental and physical abuse because it made you.
- You don't treat people with respect because it made you.
- You thrive on chaos because it made you.
- You don't help others because it made you.
- You won't give up drinking or smoking excessively because being around it made you.
- You won't distance yourself from troubled individuals because being around them made you.
- You won't be humble or apologetic when wrong because it made you.

We're all different in our own way.

1. Parents, we're different.
2. Supervisors, we're all different.
3. Leaders, we're all different.
4. Teachers, we're all different.
5. Disciplinaries, we're all different.
6. Friendships, we're all different.
7. Co-workers, we're all different.
8. Relations, we're all different.
9. Religion, Beliefs, Faith, or Enlightenment, we're all different.
10. Racist, we're all different (Please note: We're all different culturally, environmentally, socially, individuality, and in our response to racist).

*Please appreciate more than depreciate one another differences.

Woke-up _____ on ____/____/_____   M T W T F S S   Hours of sleep ____

Sunny__ Cloudy__ Rainy__ Stormy__ Lightning__ Windy__ WTHail__ Snow__ WTMother Nature__

TODAY, I AM

☐ GREAT / GOOD
☐ HOPEFUL / HAPPY
☐ AWESOME / ACTIVE
☐ MINDFUL / MOTIVATED
☐ BOLD / BRILLIANT
☐ ENCOURAGED / ENERGIZED

STOP

☐ GROUCHY / GUARDED
☐ HURT / HATEFUL
☐ ANGRY / ANNOYED
☐ MAD / MOODY
☐ BELLIGERENT / BITTER
☐ ENRAGED / EXHAUSTED

TODAY, I AM GRATEFUL & EXCITED ABOUT:

_____

_____

_____

_____

_____

_____

_____

_____

_____

_____

_____

_____

_____

_____

_____

_____

_____

_____

_____

LAST WORD IN ("Best Moment of Today" – "My Final Thought on Today" – "NOPE!, Never Again"):

$h!+ happeneds

☐ **Another Great Day! Making my ancestors and family proud. "I Love Me"**

Driving

Would you leave your child or partner for 3-5 years with someone else to love and watch over to live in a 3000-5000 square foot home alone overseas for a chance at $30,000-50,000? Not enough, right? $300,000-500,000 _____ maybe $3,000,000-5,000,000____?

through life

Would you leave your child or partner for 3-5 years for someone else to love and watch over while you make cents on the dollar in prison? Not enough, right?

while being mindful

Respect other people's life choices, even if their choices don't match or favor the life you prefer <u>or vice versa</u>.

- A tiny home instead of a substantial square foot home is a choice.
- Vegan instead of eating meat is a choice.
- Country living instead of city life is a choice.
- Being single instead of married is a choice.
- Renting instead of owning is a choice.
- Tech school instead of traditional university is a choice.
- Relations with a humane, kind, and loving individual instead of an individual of a specific race is a choice.
- Sober instead of drinking with others is a choice.
- Strong interpersonal belief and spirituality instead of being part of or within a religious facility or organization is a choice.
- Another religious denomination instead of your chosen denomination is a choice.
- Nomad and "off the grid" living instead of a 9-5 lifestyle is a choice.
- Political participation, affiliation, and party instead of what you've chosen is a choice.

<u>Life Assurance coverage is needed</u> (free -no cost)

If someone is living a foul, hateful, and chanced lifestyle with criminality and incarceration assured; respect your life choice of living the opposite as a productive citizen with opportunity, and freedom assured.

A commendable part of a nomad life

See No Evil, Hear No Evil: It's good to know what's happening around you but sometimes we know too much about stranger's personal lives more than the individuals that are a part of our lives. Would our conversations be less interesting if we didn't discuss criminals, celebrities, influencers, and the politicians the news and social platforms put forward? Are you a celebrity gossiper who spread it to the masses but not getting paid? Do you know more of an entertainer's life than your child's friendship interactions away from home or online? Are you focused on the restaurant visited and dishes other than yours? Are you encouraged to increase your credit card balance after viewing the vacation, new purchase, or wonderful portrayed lifestyle of someone you want to be or have others believe you to be?

Woke-up _____ on _____/_____/_____   M T W T F S S   Hours of sleep _____

Sunny__ Cloudy__ Rainy__ Stormy__ Lightning__ Windy__ WTHail__ Snow__ WTMother Nature__

TODAY, I AM

☐	☐	☐	☐	☐	☐	STOP	☐	☐	☐	☐	☐	☐
GREAT	HOPEFUL	AWESOME	MINDFUL	BOLD	ENCOURAGED		GROUCHY	HURT	ANGRY	MAD	BELLIGERENT	ENRAGED
GOOD	HAPPY	ACTIVE	MOTIVATED	BRILLIANT	ENERGIZED		GUARDED	HATEFUL	ANNOYED	MOODY	BITTER	EXHAUSTED

TODAY, I AM GRATEFUL & EXCITED ABOUT:

_____

_____
_____
_____
_____
_____
_____
_____
_____
_____
_____
_____
_____
_____
_____
_____
_____
_____
_____
_____
_____
_____
_____
_____
_____

LAST WORD IN ("Best Moment of Today" – "My Final Thought on Today" – "NOPE!, Never Again"):

$h!+ happeneds

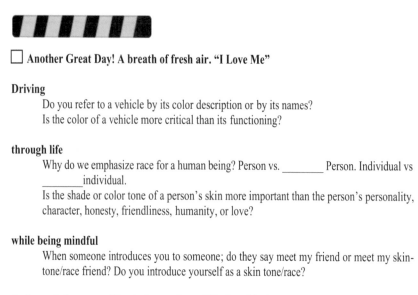

☐ **Another Great Day! A breath of fresh air. "I Love Me"**

Driving

Do you refer to a vehicle by its color description or by its names?
Is the color of a vehicle more critical than its functioning?

through life

Why do we emphasize race for a human being? Person vs. _____ Person. Individual vs _____ individual.
Is the shade or color tone of a person's skin more important than the person's personality, character, honesty, friendliness, humanity, or love?

while being mindful

When someone introduces you to someone; do they say meet my friend or meet my skin-tone/race friend? Do you introduce yourself as a skin tone/race?

A change in how something is done today will be how it's done tomorrow.
Krazy krazy Krazy (~~KkK~~) can evolve to be Keeping Kindness Kindred
Black Lives Matter (BLM) can evolve to be Because Life/Lives Matters

If blacks can install bright white or colorful light changing religious crosses in their front lawn after a history of burning crosses being used for fear and intimidation; change is possible.

If whites can be in favor of voting a black man in as the U.S. President and be in outrage of a senseless murder of an unarmed black man by an officer kneeling his neck; change is possible.

What's up with US?

Why are we still being distracted by federal figure heads antics and comments while states representatives change state laws to shield professional office duties as personal and test authoritarian power grab laws to strengthen or guarantee political parties control and re-election assurance (i.e., voting rights).

<u>Same plan working like a charm for the separators and instigator within the politics of US</u>:

Create a racial or economic distraction while passing or changing a law at lowest level to access citizen's awareness, care, push back, or support before next state or federal level.

<u>US must evolve into US</u>

A United States with a United Society, Unfaltering Spirit, Unfiltered System, Unified Sensibility with an Unstoppable SCOTUS with different interpretation, interpretation, interpretation, interpretation, interpretation, simplification, clarification, expounding, and judgment made.

Woke-up _____ on ____ / ____ / _____   M T W T F S S   Hours of sleep ____

Sunny__ Cloudy__ Rainy__ Stormy__ Lightning__ Windy__ WTHail__ Snow__ WTMother Nature__

TODAY, I AM

☐	☐	☐	☐	☐	☐	STOP	☐	☐	☐	☐	☐	☐
GREAT	HOPEFUL	AWESOME	MINDFUL	BOLD	ENCOURAGED		GROUCHY	HURT	ANGRY	MAD	BELLIGERENT	ENRAGED
GOOD	HAPPY	ACTIVE	MOTIVATED	BRILLIANT	ENERGIZED		GUARDED	HATEFUL	ANNOYED	MOODY	BITTER	EXHAUSTED

TODAY, I AM GRATEFUL & EXCITED ABOUT:

_____

_____

_____

_____

_____

_____

_____

_____

_____

_____

_____

_____

_____

_____

_____

_____

_____

_____

_____

_____

_____

_____

LAST WORD IN ("Best Moment of Today" – "My Final Thought on Today" – "NOPE!, Never Again"):

$h!+ happeneds

☐ **Another Great Day! I can't stop now. I still got this. "I Love Me"**

Driving

The gas and brake pedals will always be a little touchy and different for each vehicle. No matter how many vehicles you drive, the touchiness level of the pedals can vary. The only way you can tell if the gas or brake pedal is sensitive to you is to be in the driver's seat. The slightest touch of the gas pedal can cause a vehicle to accelerate like you put your foot into it, and the slightest touch of the brake pedal can cause your head to snap forward.

through life

Damage to friendship can happen unintentionally and in humor. It doesn't matter if you thought it was a joke; it was taken seriously. Everyone can be a little touchy, so try not to offend ONE- (a: being one in particular: being the same in kind or quality.) You won't realize how sensitive someone is until you've gone too far and offended. A sensitive person could take things personally and be provoked to respond with an unsuspecting and overwhelming attitude or action.

while being mindful

Sometimes, the words we use without thought can be slightly abrasive. A pause, word rearranging, and a softer tone can go a long way.

1. I understand you're a doctor, and I appreciate your recommendation, but you're not my doctor!
    a. **Rearranged:** You're not my doctor, but I understand you're a doctor, and I appreciate your recommendation.
2. I understand you're a parent, and I appreciate your concern for my future, but you're not my parent!
    a. **Rearranged:** You're not my parent, but I understand you're a parent, and I appreciate your concern for my future.

Woke-up _____ on ____/____/____   M T W T F S S   Hours of sleep ____

Sunny__ Cloudy__ Rainy__ Stormy__ Lightning__ Windy__ WTHail__ Snow__ WTMother Nature__

TODAY, I AM

☐	☐	☐	☐	☐	☐	🛑 STOP	☐	☐	☐	☐	☐	☐
GREAT	HOPEFUL	AWESOME	MINDFUL	BOLD	ENCOURAGED		GROUCHY	HURT	ANGRY	MAD	BELLIGERENT	ENRAGED
GOOD	HAPPY	ACTIVE	MOTIVATED	BRILLIANT	ENERGIZED		GUARDED	HATEFUL	ANNOYED	MOODY	BITTER	EXHAUSTED

TODAY, I AM GRATEFUL & EXCITED ABOUT:

_____

_____

_____

_____

_____

_____

_____

_____

_____

_____

_____

_____

_____

_____

_____

_____

_____

_____

_____

_____

_____

_____

_____

_____

LAST WORD IN ("Best Moment of Today" – "My Final Thought on Today" – "NOPE!, Never Again"):

$h!+ happeneds

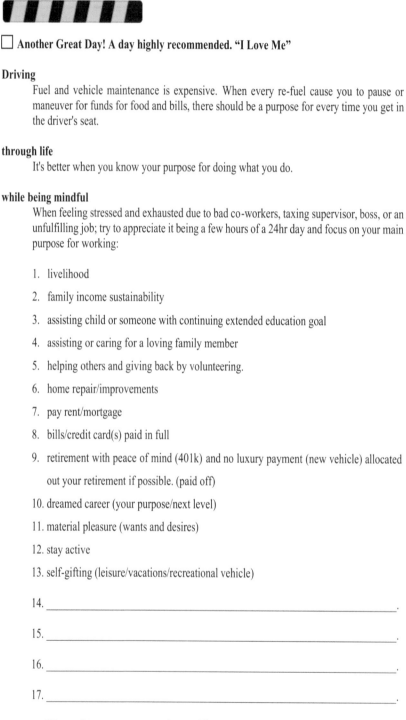

☐ **Another Great Day! A day highly recommended. "I Love Me"**

Driving

Fuel and vehicle maintenance is expensive. When every re-fuel cause you to pause or maneuver for funds for food and bills, there should be a purpose for every time you get in the driver's seat.

through life

It's better when you know your purpose for doing what you do.

while being mindful

When feeling stressed and exhausted due to bad co-workers, taxing supervisor, boss, or an unfulfilling job; try to appreciate it being a few hours of a 24hr day and focus on your main purpose for working:

1. livelihood

2. family income sustainability

3. assisting child or someone with continuing extended education goal

4. assisting or caring for a loving family member

5. helping others and giving back by volunteering.

6. home repair/improvements

7. pay rent/mortgage

8. bills/credit card(s) paid in full

9. retirement with peace of mind (401k) and no luxury payment (new vehicle) allocated out your retirement if possible. (paid off)

10. dreamed career (your purpose/next level)

11. material pleasure (wants and desires)

12. stay active

13. self-gifting (leisure/vacations/recreational vehicle)

14. _____.

15. _____.

16. _____.

17. _____.

   *Appreciate your purpose and yourself more.

Driving through life, while being mindful that

Woke-up _____ on ____/____/_____ M T W T F S S Hours of sleep ____

Sunny__ Cloudy__ Rainy__ Stormy__ Lightning__ Windy__ WTHail__ Snow__ WTMother Nature__

TODAY, I AM

☐	☐	☐	☐	☐	☐	STOP	☐	☐	☐	☐	☐	☐
GREAT	HOPEFUL	AWESOME	MINDFUL	BOLD	ENCOURAGED		GROUCHY	HURT	ANGRY	MAD	BELLIGERENT	ENRAGED
GOOD	HAPPY	ACTIVE	MOTIVATED	BRILLIANT	ENERGIZED		GUARDED	HATEFUL	ANNOYED	MOODY	BITTER	EXHAUSTED

TODAY, I AM GRATEFUL & EXCITED ABOUT:

_____

_____

_____

_____

_____

_____

_____

_____

_____

_____

_____

_____

_____

_____

_____

_____

_____

_____

_____

_____

_____

_____

_____

_____

_____

_____

LAST WORD IN ("Best Moment of Today" – "My Final Thought on Today" – "NOPE!, Never Again"):

$h!+ happeneds

☐ **Another Great Day! 10 out of 10 humans surveyed recommend it. "I Love Me"**

Driving

Stop labeling vehicles by their type or labeling people by the type of vehicle they drive.

- Sports cars are dangerous. (driver dangerous, not vehicle)
- Soccer mom drive vans (convenience)
- Older men driving sports cars are having a midlife crisis. (dream vehicle finally attainable)
- Flashy paint means flashy or self-absorb. (favorite color)

through life

A person's age, race, or nationality never determines their economics, status, potential, preferences, residency, or career; so, stop stereotyping people by their outward appearance.

while being mindful

The intended use of stereotyping is to divide, separate, belittle, group, recruit, champion, demean or hurt. Many say they never stereotype anyone or have any bias, but too many have bias fault lines systematically and covertly created deep within themselves. The invisible fault lines that result in racial tremors, misogynist aftershocks, discriminatory earthquakes, or hateful tsunamis.

Plan life accordingly (slow down or speed up): Don't misjudge your future happiness by the few out of a million who live a long life 80-100. We're all not 100 age anomalies. There's a higher propensity that your life expectancy will be like your family's or environmental average. If your family lineage tops out at 70 yrs. old; your middle age number is 35. **"Keep it 100"**

Woke-up _____ on _____/_____/_____   M T W T F S S   Hours of sleep ____

Sunny__ Cloudy__ Rainy__ Stormy__   Lightning__ Windy__ WTHail__ Snow__ WTMother Nature__

TODAY, I AM

☐ GREAT ☐ HOPEFUL ☐ AWESOME ☐ MINDFUL ☐ BOLD ☐ ENCOURAGED   **STOP**   ☐ GROUCHY ☐ HURT ☐ ANGRY ☐ MAD ☐ BELLIGERENT ☐ ENRAGED

GOOD   HAPPY   ACTIVE   MOTIVATED BRILLIANT ENERGIZED | GUARDED   HATEFUL ANNOYED MOODY   BITTER EXHAUSTED

TODAY, I AM GRATEFUL & EXCITED ABOUT:

_____

_____

_____

_____

_____

_____

_____

_____

_____

_____

_____

_____

_____

_____

_____

_____

_____

_____

_____

_____

_____

_____

_____

_____

LAST WORD IN ("Best Moment of Today" – "My Final Thought on Today" – "NOPE!, Never Again"):

$h!+ happeneds

For Parents & Legal Guardians
A youth's check on living and race relations awareness questions to gauge, discuss, and talk.

1. What is the first profession you think of if I say I'm Caucasian and my profession involves me dressing professionally in court? _____ Why that answer?

2. What is the first profession you think of if I say I'm Hispanic and my profession involves me being outside most of my workday? _____ Why that answer?

3. What is the first profession you think of if I say I'm Black and my profession involves drug making and distribution? _____ Why that answer?

4. What is the first profession you think of if I say I'm Asian and my profession involves using my hands? _____ Why that answer?

5. What is the first profession you think of if I say I'm Indian and my profession involves providing professional service to new and continuing customers daily? _____ Why that answer?

Youth discussion follow-up:
1. Did the youth answer humble defendant, professional criminal, bailiff, paralegal, court reporter, judge, lawyer, or assume another lesser/ higher profession?
2. Did the youth answer horticulturist, arborist, turf scientist, environmental engineer, manager, professional baseball/soccer player, landscaping business owner, geographer, park ranger, lawn care laborer, or assume another lesser/higher profession?
3. Did the youth answer doctor, pharmacist, holistic practitioner, scientist, pharmaceutical distributor, pharmacy tech, a cannabis business owner/vendor, biostatistician, illegal drug dealer, chemist, or assume another lesser/higher profession?
4. Did the youth answer doctor, nurse, chef, salon staff, construction, hand model, welder, chiropractor, architect, mechanic, sonographer, martial artist, massage therapist, or assume another lesser/ higher profession?
5. Did the youth answer doctor, franchisee, hotel entrepreneur, customer service rep convenience/gas store owner, concierge, accountant, casino owner, banker, flight attendant, receptionist, customer service manager, casino employee, or lessor/higher profession?

Exercise Purpose Only: In life; the correct answer is never to assume or answer race-baiting stereotyping conversations or questions and never add or assume race determines anyone's ability, worth aptitude, or profession.

Driving through life, while being mindful that

Woke-up _____ on ____/____/____   M T W T F S S   Hours of sleep ____

Sunny__ Cloudy__ Rainy__ Stormy__ Lightning__ Windy__ WTHail__ Snow__ WTMother Nature__

TODAY, I AM

☐	☐	☐	☐	☐	☐	STOP	☐	☐	☐	☐	☐	☐
GREAT	HOPEFUL	AWESOME	MINDFUL	BOLD	ENCOURAGED		GROUCHY	HURT	ANGRY	MAD	BELLIGERENT	ENRAGED
GOOD	HAPPY	ACTIVE	MOTIVATED	BRILLIANT	ENERGIZED		GUARDED	HATEFUL	ANNOYED	MOODY	BITTER	EXHAUSTED

TODAY, I AM GRATEFUL & EXCITED ABOUT:

_____

_____
_____
_____
_____
_____
_____
_____
_____
_____
_____
_____
_____
_____
_____
_____
_____
_____
_____
_____
_____
_____
_____
_____
_____

LAST WORD IN ("Best Moment of Today" – "My Final Thought on Today" – "NOPE!, Never Again"):

$h!+ happeneds

☐ **Another Great Day! Don't take this day the wrong way. "I Love Me"**

Driving

It happens to us all.

- You'll be driving to an important destination, every traffic light will be red, and all traffic will seem to be against you.

    or

- You'll be driving to an important destination, every traffic light will be green, and all traffic will be in your favor.

through life

It happens to us all.

- Wrong Place-Bad Timing (missed opportunity)

    or

- Right Place- Perfect Timing (on point).

while being mindful

Hearsay's evidence isn't deemed admissible in a court of law, but it was allowed to shape, persuade, and deceive a society of people for a racial power structure. Most of what we know as our learned truth is "hearsay." We've been told of unproven feats, unreliable tales, and secondhand stories by an unchecked, unbalanced, and unwavering power structure that still feels threatened by anyone's truthful testimony, evidence collection, history validation, and society's humane awakening and unification.

It is hard for someone to know of you or how you feel without experiencing as you do.

In court, legal testimony given by two individuals with slight similarities and omissions in their statements is more believable than if their statements match word for word. In American history books, the history of slavery told and written as factual (hypothesizing) by WHAAATE or IHAAATE People and slave owners with slight similarities and blatant omissions in their recollections are more believable than a non-white's and non-WHAAATE's book, if their facts and recollections of slavery and Jim Crow era hatred had match word for word or similar.

ONE TEAM - ONE DREAM TEAM

To resist past hate's return and it's repugnance and to foster a cohesive and loving world, society needs a team of citizens to join forces to make up the **"ONE TEAM"** (America's Dream Team):

- ☑ One team of citizens must be **W**hole**h**eartedly **i**nclusive **t**o an **e**qual **S**ociety.

- ☑ One team must have strong and cohesive **B**eliefs, **l**eaders, **a**ttitude, **C**ommitment, **k**indness, and be **S**pirited.

- ☑ And last team must be **O**verseers **t**o **h**elp **e**radicated **r**acist **S**ystems (education, housing, politics, citizenship, and all *finacials* acts).

FT GHAMBE

Woke-up _____ on ____/____/____ M T W T F S S Hours of sleep ____

Sunny_ Cloudy_ Rainy_ Stormy_ Lightning_ Windy_ WTHail_ Snow_ WTMother Nature_

TODAY, I AM

☐ ☐ ☐ ☐ ☐ ☐ **STOP** ☐ ☐ ☐ ☐ ☐ ☐

GREAT HOPEFUL AWESOME MINDFUL BOLD ENCOURAGED | GROUCHY HURT ANGRY MAD BELLIGERENT ENRAGED

GOOD HAPPY ACTIVE MOTIVATED BRILLIANT ENERGIZED | GUARDED HATEFUL ANNOYED MOODY BITTER EXHAUSTED

TODAY, I AM GRATEFUL & EXCITED ABOUT:

_____

_____

_____

_____

_____

_____

_____

_____

_____

_____

_____

_____

_____

_____

_____

_____

_____

_____

_____

_____

_____

LAST WORD IN ("Best Moment of Today" – "My Final Thought on Today" – "NOPE!, Never Again"):

$h!+ happeneds

☐ **Another Great Day! Awesome. Just like last year this time. "I Love Me"**

Driving

Even with all the technological advancements, no vehicle can run without refueling or recharging.

through life

Even with all the medical advancements, there's no better medicine than mental and physical rest. <u>Caffeinated High Reminder:</u> For every hour a caffeinated energy drink, supplement or shot keeps you awake, that same hour must be recuperated and recouped back. Drinks and drug stimulants used to keep you awake only delay the rest your body needs.

while being mindful

Take care of your one body. Body freezing (cryo-assoffonics) is a way-out thought or a way-out reality in an alternative realm or universe.

When was your last medical checkup or physical?

Don't be like some individuals who get their vehicle maintenance check-ups and servicing done more than they do for their body.

Woke-up _____ on ____/____/____ M T W T F S S Hours of sleep ____

Sunny__ Cloudy__ Rainy__ Stormy__ Lightning__ Windy__ WTHail__ Snow__ WTMother Nature__

TODAY, I AM

☐ ☐ ☐ ☐ ☐ ☐ **STOP** ☐ ☐ ☐ ☐ ☐ ☐

| GREAT | HOPEFUL | AWESOME | MINDFUL | BOLD | ENCOURAGED | | GROUCHY | HURT | ANGRY | MAD | BELLIGERENT | ENRAGED |
| GOOD | HAPPY | ACTIVE | MOTIVATED | BRILLIANT | ENERGIZED | | GUARDED | HATEFUL | ANNOYED | MOODY | BITTER | EXHAUSTED |

TODAY, I AM GRATEFUL & EXCITED ABOUT:

_____

_____

_____

_____

_____

_____

_____

_____

_____

_____

_____

_____

_____

_____

_____

_____

_____

_____

_____

_____

_____

_____

_____

_____

_____

LAST WORD IN ("Best Moment of Today" – "My Final Thought on Today" – "NOPE!, Never Again"):

$h!+ happeneds

☐ **Another Great Day! I would like to thank me for being present today. "I Love Me"**

$h!+ can go astray quickly from doing mischief and dumb $h!+

Life Incident #1: Lying, Secretive, Evasive, Disrespectful, & Disappears
Probable Cause: Young, Associates, Discipline, Minimal Parental Guidance/Time
Charges: "Young & Clueless"
System: Parents
Disposition: Talk/ Grounding / Failing classes / Loss of Privileges/Allowance, No Cellphone / Electronics / Computer use /After School /Detention / Juvenile Detention
Worst Case probability: Loss of trust / Run away / Trafficked

Life Incident #2: Report of weapons and drugs on the school ground.
Probable Cause: Proximity, Past Actions, Friend, Associations, Gossip
Charges: Drugs/Dangerous weapons on school grounds
System: School Board-Judicial
Disposition: Suspension-Arrest
Worst Case probability: Drug Program / Expulsion / Youth Detention Center / Criminal Record (1st Offender hopefully) /Meet with Counseling or Psychiatry

Life Incident #3 (Bolo) "Be on the lookout" for 3 teenage boys leaving the store suspected of shoplifting.
Probable Cause: Report of shoplifting
Charges: Shoplifting
System: Police-Juvenile Court
Disposition: Guilty, First Offender or Probation
Worst Case probability: Youth Detention Center / Jail / Criminal Record (College Acceptance or Career Hindrance.
Reality: Only one shoplifted, but all three were arrested and stigmatized.
  1. Two were unaware of theft, but will the legal system believe they were not aware?
  2. Is there any evidence, eyewitness, or surveillance available to clear the two innocents? If so, will their innocence and having no knowledge be believed?
  3. Many trusted friendships deteriorated because of one's selfishness and disrespect of anyone other than themselves. Sadly, most frenemies are usually revealed at the wrong "Dagnabbit" time.

A Traffic Stop Probability:
Probable Cause: Headlight requirement-No headlights on the half-hour after sunset. (FT GHAMBE GA 40-8-20)
Charges: Headlight, no seatbelt, no proof of insurance, expired registration, and DUI?
System: Court
Disposition: Ticket, guilty, suspended license, fined, driver's license points, arrest, probation, first offender. Not Death.
Worst Case probability: Failure to appear> warrant> extended time in jail>harmed, loss of job/income, or *death.*

Driving through life, while being mindful that

Woke-up _____ on ____/____/____ M T W T F S S Hours of sleep ____

Sunny__ Cloudy__ Rainy__ Stormy__ Lightning__ Windy__ WTHail__ Snow__ WTMother Nature__

TODAY, I AM

GREAT	HOPEFUL	AWESOME	MINDFUL	BOLD	ENCOURAGED	STOP	GROUCHY	HURT	ANGRY	MAD	BELLIGERENT	ENRAGED

GOOD   HAPPY   ACTIVE   MOTIVATED BRILLIANT ENERGIZED   GUARDED HATEFUL ANNOYED MOODY BITTER EXHAUSTED

TODAY, I AM GRATEFUL & EXCITED ABOUT:

_____
_____
_____
_____
_____
_____
_____
_____
_____
_____
_____
_____
_____
_____
_____
_____
_____
_____
_____
_____
_____
_____
_____

LAST WORD IN ("Best Moment of Today" – "My Final Thought on Today" – "NOPE!, Never Again"):

$h!+ happeneds

☐ **Another Great Day! My unspoken but favorite gifted words each day. "I Love Me"**

Driving

A traffic stops empathy pledge for citizens and law enforcers.

I promise to remain calm and respectful of your time and rights because

I AM YOU.

I have the right to be cautious, fearful, nervous, or speculative of this stop like you.

I want our interaction to go smoothly because I am you.

I want you to not fear me.

I want to drive off safely because I am you.

I want to go home and be with my family, friends, or pet(s) like you.

I appreciate life like you because I am you.

I love life.

I AM YOU.

This is my oath to you today:

Name: _____

Date: _____

Time: _____

through life

Feeling safe and being safe are not the same. Help me help us to feel safe.

while being mindful

Traffic Stop Probabilities:

Probable Cause: Headlight requirement-No headlights on the half-hour after sunset. (FT GHAMBE, GA 40-8-20) https://dps.georgia.gov/

Charges: Headlight, no seatbelt, no proof of insurance, expired registration, or DUI?

System: Court

Disposition: Ticket, guilty, suspended license, fined, driver's license points, arrest, probation, first offender. No Escalation Required. No Bravado, Not Personal. Not Death.

Worst Case probability: **Officer**: Loss of Public/Trust Relations /Case /Officer Resigns.

Citizen: Failure to appear, warrant, extended time in jail, loss of job/income, or death.

Driving through life, while being mindful that

Woke-up _____ on ____ / ____ / ____   M T W T F S S   Hours of sleep ____

Sunny__ Cloudy__ Rainy__ Stormy__ Lightning__ Windy__ WTHail__ Snow__ WTMother Nature__

TODAY, I AM

☐	☐	☐	☐	☐	☐	**STOP**	☐	☐	☐	☐	☐	☐
GREAT	HOPEFUL	AWESOME	MINDFUL	BOLD	ENCOURAGED		GROUCHY	HURT	ANGRY	MAD	BELLIGERENT	ENRAGED
GOOD	HAPPY	ACTIVE	MOTIVATED	BRILLIANT	ENERGIZED		GUARDED	HATEFUL	ANNOYED	MOODY	BITTER	EXHAUSTED

TODAY, I AM GRATEFUL & EXCITED ABOUT:

_____

_____
_____
_____
_____
_____
_____
_____
_____
_____
_____
_____
_____
_____
_____
_____
_____
_____
_____
_____
_____
_____
_____

LAST WORD IN ("Best Moment of Today" – "My Final Thought on Today" – "NOPE!, Never Again"):

$h!+ happeneds

☐ **Another Great Day! Rejoice. It's a Wonderful Day-Life. "I Love Me"**

Driving

What's the smart and safest thing to do if someone rolls up blasting music you don't like? Never allow yourself to become irritated by another driver's driving, where their actions control your driving. When law enforcement arrives, two individuals or parties are usually at the scene of a reported road rage incident, both are either titled a victim or subject, injured or aggressor, released or arrested, or deceased or killer. -Choose wisely-

through life

What's the smartest and safest thing to do if someone steps up to you using profanity and hateful words you don't like? Don't speak the same. Don't lose your life over something non-consequential to your life as a disagreement. Walk away and look forward to a better day ahead. No one continues to argue with themselves, and if they do continue, excellent job distancing yourself from the real issue, they need to be concerned with.

while being mindful

An argument is like an individual passing wind (flatulence) in the presence of strangers.
- expected
- embarrassing
- sometimes viewed as immaturity
- irritating
- maybe a warning signs for more to follow
- part of life
- may be preventable to a degree (listen/lactose)
- fills the air and takes over a room
- sometimes noticeable and sometimes not
- it's only a thing when someone else is involved (catches wind of it).

Basic Combative Person Fundamentals (no weapons involved or required):

<u>Steady Your Position</u> – don't engage or reciprocate the same.
<u>Aim</u> – align mental calm and focus on resolving the issue without violence.
<u>Breathing</u> – controls your temperament.
<u>Press-on</u> – be silent, de-escalate, or remove yourself without engagement.

* Arguments are not worth your lifetime; so, value your time, livelihood, and life accordingly.

Woke-up _____ on ____/____/____   M T W T F S S   Hours of sleep ____

Sunny__ Cloudy__ Rainy__ Stormy__ Lightning__ Windy__ WTHail__ Snow__ WTMother Nature__

TODAY, I AM

☐	☐	☐	☐	☐	☐	STOP	☐	☐	☐	☐	☐	☐
GREAT	HOPEFUL	AWESOME	MINDFUL	BOLD	ENCOURAGED		GROUCHY	HURT	ANGRY	MAD	BELLIGERENT	ENRAGED
GOOD	HAPPY	ACTIVE	MOTIVATED	BRILLIANT	ENERGIZED		GUARDED	HATEFUL	ANNOYED	MOODY	BITTER	EXHAUSTED

TODAY, I AM GRATEFUL & EXCITED ABOUT:

_____

_____
_____
_____
_____
_____
_____
_____
_____
_____
_____
_____
_____
_____
_____
_____
_____
_____
_____
_____
_____
_____
_____
_____

LAST WORD IN ("Best Moment of Today" – "My Final Thought on Today" – "NOPE!, Never Again"):

$h!+ happeneds

☐ **Another Great Day! Yes, sumptuously grand but affordable. "I Love Me"**

Driving

Be cautious when refueling your vehicle.

- Is there a key fob or key left in the ignition?
- Is someone coming near to ask or discuss to distract you from another's action?
- Is there a baby or small child vulnerable to being taken in a carjacking?
- Is there a cellular device, itinerary, passport, luggage, wallet, or purse visible and easily accessible?
- Is there a tempting item for an opportunist?

through life

Something small to you is advantageous to someone looking to do you wrong. Be cautious of what's displayed inside your purse or wallet when opening it in the presence of strangers:

- Have awareness of the photos you're displaying unless you're aware and displaying fakeness to confuse or warn.
- Are your financial cards, military ID, access badge, or cash on hand visible? Flip-it
- Could someone recognize if you're local, a visitor, or foreigner?
- Could someone determine your location by a visible driver's license or hotel room key card?
- Does your key fob inform someone of your vehicle's make?
- Does you carry conceal permit inform someone there's a weapon to grab in your vehicle or room.

while being mindful

A small object on the floor is enormous to a crawling baby or pet. Something small and inconsequential to you is humongous and valuable to a criminal plotting, monitoring, and convinced of an easy target.

Phones/Laptops tidbits:

- Always assume a camera or criminal is recording. Be cautious who's visible when you're entering your password and passcode. You could be the individual on display while someone is appearing or portraying, they're doing face time with another or doing a selfie.
- Don't let the visibility of cameras, crowd, and staff members make you overconfidence about your electronic device use and security.

Bags, Purses, and Backpacks tidbit:

- Keep them in front of you or someone watching and covering you six and your four through eight blind spots. Stop hanging them on the back of chairs out of your visual. Some individual asking a question, hustling, or sparking conversation could be the distractor. Making Groceries: Shoppers, please stop leaving open purses in shopping carts hoping criminals are taking a day off.

Woke-up _____ on ____/____/____   M T W T F S S   Hours of sleep ____

Sunny__ Cloudy__ Rainy__ Stormy__ Lightning__ Windy__ WTHail__ Snow__ WTMother Nature__

TODAY, I AM

☐ ☐ ☐ ☐ ☐ ☐ **STOP** ☐ ☐ ☐ ☐ ☐ ☐

| GREAT | HOPEFUL | AWESOME | MINDFUL | BOLD | ENCOURAGED | | GROUCHY | HURT | ANGRY | MAD | BELLIGERENT | ENRAGED |
| GOOD | HAPPY | ACTIVE | MOTIVATED | BRILLIANT | ENERGIZED | | GUARDED | HATEFUL | ANNOYED | MOODY | BITTER | EXHAUSTED |

TODAY, I AM GRATEFUL & EXCITED ABOUT:

_____

_____

_____

_____

_____

_____

_____

_____

_____

_____

_____

_____

_____

_____

_____

_____

_____

_____

_____

_____

_____

_____

_____

LAST WORD IN ("Best Moment of Today" – "My Final Thought on Today" – "NOPE!, Never Again"):

$h!+ happeneds

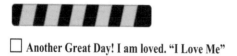

☐ **Another Great Day! I am loved. "I Love Me"**

Driving

Expect to see vehicles weave in and out of traffic but go no further in traffic.

through life

Expect to come across many who give an appearance they are doing a lot and further than most, but they are not.

while being mindful

Are you 100% sure of what you say, believe, or go against of another?
What makes your less than 100% unproven truthfulness more valid, valuable, or higher percentage of another's truthfulness?

No story is told the same, and no story is believed the same.
1. You are smarter than me.
2. You know more than me.
3. You are more than that.

Woke-up _____ on _____/_____/_____   M T W T F S S   Hours of sleep _____

Sunny__ Cloudy__ Rainy__ Stormy__ Lightning__ Windy__ WTHail__ Snow__ WTMother Nature__

TODAY, I AM

☐	☐	☐	☐	☐	☐	🛑	☐	☐	☐	☐	☐	☐
GREAT	HOPEFUL	AWESOME	MINDFUL	BOLD	ENCOURAGED		GROUCHY	HURT	ANGRY	MAD	BELLIGERENT	ENRAGED
GOOD	HAPPY	ACTIVE	MOTIVATED	BRILLIANT	ENERGIZED		GUARDED	HATEFUL	ANNOYED	MOODY	BITTER	EXHAUSTED

TODAY, I AM GRATEFUL & EXCITED ABOUT:

_____

_____
_____
_____
_____
_____
_____
_____
_____
_____
_____
_____
_____
_____
_____
_____
_____
_____
_____
_____
_____
_____
_____
_____
_____

LAST WORD IN ("Best Moment of Today" – "My Final Thought on Today" – "NOPE!, Never Again"):

$h!+ happeneds

☐ **Another Great Day! Take a bow. "I Love Me"**

Driving

You will not know how strong the vehicle chassis is until you drive with some weight. You must know how much weight your vehicle can sustain to operate safely. The vehicle chassis consists of an internal frame and understructure that supports the most integral components, body, engines, circuitry, and passenger(s). Chassis of varied sizes are built to handle a designated weight limit and nothing more. Too much weight in the vehicle will cause the engine to work harder, lead to more wear on the suspension, axle, and tires, and potentially cause the chassis to collapse.

through life

You can only bear so much. Of course, we differ from person to person, but theoretically, everyone is expected to handle more than they think they can handle. While it is commendable that some will try to handle more on their own, it is more commendable to seek assistance and guidance before becoming overwhelmed. Most believe a person's breakdown is triggered by one major catastrophic event or numerous minor stressful incidents, but the reality is that it could happen anytime or by anything. It would be best if you never assumed what's minimal to you is not significant, monumental, or catastrophic to another.

while being mindful

Some relationships are like losing weight. You hope to get back to the way things were, but:

- there's no signs of improvement or change.
- things don't happen overnight or quickly and require time, effort, and patience.
- things get worse and weigh you down more.
- things can start affecting your health.
- things went back to the same after a few months.
- things don't fit right anymore and it maybe time to change out the old for the new.

Woke-up _____ on ____/_____/_____   M T W T F S S   Hours of sleep ____

Sunny__ Cloudy__ Rainy__ Stormy__ Lightning__ Windy__ WTHail__ Snow__ WTMother Nature__

TODAY, I AM

☐	☐	☐	☐	☐	☐	STOP	☐	☐	☐	☐	☐	☐
GREAT	HOPEFUL	AWESOME	MINDFUL	BOLD	ENCOURAGED		GROUCHY	HURT	ANGRY	MAD	BELLIGERENT	ENRAGED
GOOD	HAPPY	ACTIVE	MOTIVATED	BRILLIANT	ENERGIZED		GUARDED	HATEFUL	ANNOYED	MOODY	BITTER	EXHAUSTED

TODAY, I AM GRATEFUL & EXCITED ABOUT:

_____

_____
_____
_____
_____
_____
_____
_____
_____
_____
_____
_____
_____
_____
_____
_____
_____
_____
_____
_____
_____
_____
_____
_____
_____

LAST WORD IN ("Best Moment of Today" – "My Final Thought on Today" – "NOPE!, Never Again"):

$h!+ happeneds

☐ **Oh, my goodness. Another Great Day! "I Love Me"**

Driving

A posted sign that warns you "NO PARKING AFTER FIVE O'CLOCK" is better than being ticketed or towed for no reason.

through life

Knowing about your partner's likes, dislikes, and their point of no return at the earliest is better than your partner being at their wit's end and walking out on you.

while being mindful

Relationship wisdom is having an all-knowing and keen sense of a partner's answer instead of questioning or deciding your best answer. It's in your best peaceful interest to set your likes and dislike tone early with your partner so that everyone enjoys your level of harmony. What every relationship partner needs to know:

1. Know what you allow is need. (personal time/space)

2. Know what you consider disrespectful.

3. Know if you can be trusted.

4. Know if you're dependable.

5. Know if you listen, interrupt, or have selective hearing deficiencies)

6. Know when, where, and what time to call you. (availability)

7. Know what you're okay with or not (spicy food/types of cuisines/allergies).

8. Know how something makes you feel (no or yes response, groups, ex-baggage, kids).

9. Know if you need space (too soon/too much).

10. Know what you desire or agree upon. (relationships title or not)

11. Know if you are involved with another. (inclusive/exclusive).

12. Know if you both have the same or similar interests. (religion, family, friends, music, or movies).

13. Know if you are open-minded to their likes, concerns, or thoughts. (gauging if you're the same or different than their last)

Woke-up _____ on ____/____/____   M T W T F S S   Hours of sleep ____

Sunny__ Cloudy__ Rainy__ Stormy__ Lightning__ Windy__ WTHail__ Snow__ WTMother Nature__

TODAY, I AM

☐	☐	☐	☐	☐	☐	STOP	☐	☐	☐	☐	☐	☐
GREAT	HOPEFUL	AWESOME	MINDFUL	BOLD	ENCOURAGED		GROUCHY	HURT	ANGRY	MAD	BELLIGERENT	ENRAGED
GOOD	HAPPY	ACTIVE	MOTIVATED	BRILLIANT	ENERGIZED		GUARDED	HATEFUL	ANNOYED	MOODY	BITTER	EXHAUSTED

TODAY, I AM GRATEFUL & EXCITED ABOUT:

_____

_____
_____
_____
_____
_____
_____
_____
_____
_____
_____
_____
_____
_____
_____
_____
_____
_____
_____
_____
_____
_____
_____
_____
_____

LAST WORD IN ("Best Moment of Today" – "My Final Thought on Today" – "NOPE!, Never Again"):

$h!+ happeneds

☐ **Another Great Day! Superb. "I Love Me"**

Driving

If you observe a vehicle suspected of being involved in a child's abduction, amber alert, and all other alerts, please don't stay silent.

through life

If you observe an adult's interaction or involvement with a child being odd, suspicious, or unlawful, please don't stay silent.

while being mindful

There is never a time when an adult should stop and ask a child for direction or assistance, especially today with cell phones, navigation systems, and other adults of the area or world readily available. **Never ever, EVER-EVER.**

FT GHAMBE

Woke-up _____ on ____ / ____ / _____   M T W T F S S   Hours of sleep ____

Sunny__ Cloudy__ Rainy__ Stormy__ Lightning__ Windy__ WTHail__ Snow__ WTMother Nature__

TODAY, I AM

☐	☐	☐	☐	☐	☐	STOP	☐	☐	☐	☐	☐	☐
GREAT	HOPEFUL	AWESOME	MINDFUL	BOLD	ENCOURAGED		GROUCHY	HURT	ANGRY	MAD	BELLIGERENT	ENRAGED
GOOD	HAPPY	ACTIVE	MOTIVATED	BRILLIANT	ENERGIZED		GUARDED	HATEFUL	ANNOYED	MOODY	BITTER	EXHAUSTED

TODAY, I AM GRATEFUL & EXCITED ABOUT:

_____

_____
_____
_____
_____
_____
_____
_____
_____
_____
_____
_____
_____
_____
_____
_____
_____
_____
_____
_____
_____
_____
_____
_____
_____

LAST WORD IN ("Best Moment of Today" – "My Final Thought on Today" – "NOPE!, Never Again"):

$h!+ happeneds

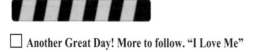

☐ **Another Great Day! More to follow. "I Love Me"**

Driving

Some driver errors can be faulted to a driver's experience (learner's permit), but not if they're with a valid permit. Just because you did it before does not mean the results, reaction, response, or consequences will be the same the next time.

through life

One significant difference between any set of rules is the consequences for not following those rules.

"Don't get it twisted."

1. "That prank was funny in high school and among your friends, but the same prank will get you fired from your job."
2. "What you did in secret before joining the military will get you kicked out of the military."
3. "A misdemeanor in one state is a felony conviction in another."
4. "That hate you spewed amongst buddies is always disrespectful to all others."
5. "This is not your parent's house or your house; you're a guest."
6. "That's what they allowed you to do, but I am not them."
7. "Yes, that first-time verbal warning was your only warning."
8. "That's how you did it there, but this is how we do it here."

while being mindful

1. One "N" word? I can understand being disappointed in an individual's use of it but don't let a disrespectful and angry word imposed onto you from the past change your future and have you in the hospital or jail angrier.
2. N!gg* is a negative word, used to create an unfavorable reaction. It is a negative word that is never good to say or put in writing, even for those you would be presumed to be okay or use the words. A darker skin-tone person saying the "N" word to one another doesn't take the bite out of the word. Only a person not using the word takes the bite out of the word. Try using "What's up given name? "Vipi! my friend?"
3. Suggestion: If you're ever referred to as a N!gg* for a negative response, always give the individual the muted response. Never lose mental control over your physicality when responding to a non-physical overture and hate-baiting individual BUT if they continue to mispronounce the word and you so desire (last resort) to correct their misspelling or pronunciation, respond with Niger along with some detailed information about Niger, (read up to share when you hear its mispronunciation). Don't lose your freedom over a word you didn't create or developed

Five additional responses when the Negativity word ("N!nj@" word) is directed toward you.

1. Yes. Niger is in West Africa and its home to the largest protected area in Africa.
2. Incorrect, Niger people are called Nigerians. Niger comes from the Niger River.
3. Close. The word you're try of pronunciation correctly is Negate, Niagara, or Negra (Spanish).
4. Yes, I have been informed that I am of African royalty?
5. Congrats, you figured me out, I am negative toward negative individuals as you.

Driving through life, while being mindful that

Woke-up _____ on ____/_____/_____   M T W T F S S   Hours of sleep ____

Sunny__ Cloudy__ Rainy__ Stormy__ Lightning__ Windy__ WTHail__ Snow__ WTMother Nature__

TODAY, I AM

☐ ☐ ☐ ☐ ☐ ☐ **STOP** ☐ ☐ ☐ ☐ ☐ ☐

GREAT	HOPEFUL	AWESOME	MINDFUL	BOLD	ENCOURAGED		GROUCHY	HURT	ANGRY	MAD	BELLIGERENT	ENRAGED
GOOD	HAPPY	ACTIVE	MOTIVATED	BRILLIANT	ENERGIZED		GUARDED	HATEFUL	ANNOYED	MOODY	BITTER	EXHAUSTED

TODAY, I AM GRATEFUL & EXCITED ABOUT:

_____

_____

_____

_____

_____

_____

_____

_____

_____

_____

_____

_____

_____

_____

_____

_____

_____

_____

_____

_____

_____

_____

_____

_____

LAST WORD IN ("Best Moment of Today" – "My Final Thought on Today" – "NOPE!, Never Again"):

$h!+ happeneds

☐ **Another Great Day! A natural high (no substances needed). "I Love Me"**

Driving

Trusting a Designated Driver (DD): How would you know if you're safe with a sober or inebriated Designated Driver if you are under the influence or passed out?

through life

Trustworthiness must be earned and treasured; not levied, automatic, guaranteed, or assumed.

while being mindful

For the exhausted few (author included). Stop wasting energy on speculation, hypotheticals, assumptions, eavesdrops, rumors and deep conspiracy theories, or you won't have the energy to trust when needed.

We all trust others and many unknowns more than we can fathom.

- We assume trust in all we purchase and consume. We assume trust in alcoholic beverages because we automatically trust farmers, manufacturers, distilleries, FDA, labelers, mixologists, party hosts, and bartenders.
- We assume trust in eating out because no customer enters the restaurant's kitchen to inspect how and who's preparing or cooking.
- We trust other drivers to drive on their side of the lane or maintain their lane if travelling in the same or opposite direction.

Finagling Drug Accountability (FDA) Questionnaire

1. Why isn't there fanfare of who is appointed to the **U.S.** Department of Health & Human Services Finagling Drug Accountability?
2. Who approves the food and drugs that the President, Vice-President, Congress, Federal Judges, Service Members, and YOU consume?
3. Why isn't there as much scrutinizing, monitoring, or request for transparency regarding FDA's life-altering decisions?
4. Who can overrule FDA's approval?
5. Can a pharmaceutical company become a billion-dollar conglomerate without the FDA?
6. Who would be the best ex-employee for a pharmaceutical company?

Woke-up _____ on ____/_____/_____   M T W T F S S   Hours of sleep ____

Sunny__ Cloudy__ Rainy__ Stormy__ Lightning__ Windy__ WTHail__ Snow__ WTMother Nature__

TODAY, I AM

☐ GREAT ☐ HOPEFUL ☐ AWESOME ☐ MINDFUL ☐ BOLD ☐ ENCOURAGED **STOP** ☐ GROUCHY ☐ HURT ☐ ANGRY ☐ MAD ☐ BELLIGERENT ☐ ENRAGED

GOOD HAPPY ACTIVE MOTIVATED BRILLIANT ENERGIZED | GUARDED HATEFUL ANNOYED MOODY BITTER EXHAUSTED

TODAY, I AM GRATEFUL & EXCITED ABOUT:

_____

_____

_____

_____

_____

_____

_____

_____

_____

_____

_____

_____

_____

_____

_____

_____

_____

_____

_____

_____

_____

_____

_____

_____

_____

LAST WORD IN ("Best Moment of Today" – "My Final Thought on Today" – "NOPE!, Never Again"):

$h!+ happeneds

☐ **Another Great Day! Solid. "I Love Me"**

The "RACE" word:

When you hear "race," should you immediately think or feel you're competing against someone or something?

Why doesn't someone ask you if you like to race, go to the race, or like a certain race before asking, "What's your race?" or "What race do you identify yourself as?" first??

Would racism be possible if we never allowed "Type of Race"?

Could future generations have a better humane race if we stop requiring" Type of Race?

Why must our ending of life be the only thing we share equally?

Passing a bills

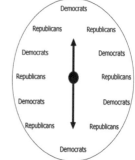

Democrat		Republican
One sided	vs	One side
Agree	vs	Disagree
We're Right	vs	We're Right
For the People (our voters)	vs	For the People (our voters)

For a bill to crossover (bipartisan)

Democrat		Republican
Quid pro Quo	vs	Quid pro Quo (What do I, my party, my bill, or my state get in return?)

What is a 50/50 chance?

Right or Wrong, Yes or No, Ying or Yang, Heads or Tails, or <u>Republican</u> or <u>Democratic</u>

while being mindful

of The *United* States? Will there ever be an option of accepting who's best for the United States, or are we destined to keep the status-quo of selecting who's loyal to a United Party with the most donations or with the most united hate, media dollars, fear warmongering or votes to defeat the opposite party, not the person? Choosing a politician in the U.S. is like taking a True or False test instead of a multiple-answered test. There will always be a 50% chance of getting the right politician in office due to the money, power, history, and media coverage going to Democrats or Republicans.

Democracy?

popular vote or popular electoral vote

popular electoral vote or popular vote of a political party in control

if Political Win- our voting democracy working

if Political Loss- our voting democracy needs to change

Is America a Democracy or Authoritarian Wanna be?

Political Power -SCOTUS lifetime appointments

Political Power -federal judges' lifetime appointments

Political Power -unlimited terms until scandal, health, or disagreement with fellow party members

Driving through life, while being mindful that

Woke-up _____ on ____/____/____   M T W T F S S   Hours of sleep ____

Sunny_   Cloudy_   Rainy_   Stormy_   Lightning_   Windy_   WTHail_   Snow_   WTMother Nature_

TODAY, I AM

☐   ☐   ☐   ☐   ☐   ☐   **STOP**   ☐   ☐   ☐   ☐   ☐   ☐

GREAT	HOPEFUL	AWESOME	MINDFUL	BOLD	ENCOURAGED		GROUCHY	HURT	ANGRY	MAD	BELLIGERENT	ENRAGED
GOOD	HAPPY	ACTIVE	MOTIVATED	BRILLIANT	ENERGIZED		GUARDED	HATEFUL	ANNOYED	MOODY	BITTER	EXHAUSTED

TODAY, I AM GRATEFUL & EXCITED ABOUT:

_____

_____

_____

_____

_____

_____

_____

_____

_____

_____

_____

_____

_____

_____

_____

_____

_____

_____

_____

_____

_____

LAST WORD IN ("Best Moment of Today" – "My Final Thought on Today" – "NOPE!, Never Again"):

_____

$h!+ happeneds

☐ Another Great Day! Cherish each day. "I Love Me"

Driving

Driving around lost in your area is not always bad because you can discover a better route or at least gain knowledge of routes not to be retaken. As soon as you know you are lost, stop, re-focus, change directions, ask for help, or travel the reverse route of your travel if possible.

through life

Learn from your mistakes. Every mistake isn't detrimental to your future. As soon as you know you made a mistake, stop, re-focus, change your way, don't repeat the mistake, and ask for forgiveness if necessary, and those affected will more than likely be more receptive.

while being mindful

Today, I am lost, but tomorrow I know another way.

The United States of Awareness

Are we in a prelude to the United States of Authoritarianism: I am BAP, I believe BIB, I believe in BP, I have faith in BP, and yes, I know ALM much as BLM but when was the start and end date of All Lives being abducted, sold, trade, chained, shipped, separated, and sold as a commodity again. Black lives that were sold and moved as livestock, enslaved, categorized, economically hinder, shunned, and involuntarily test medically, disproportionately incarcerated, and disenfranchised as not fully American (**African** Americans or **Black** Americans). I believe in **US**. I was born and raised in **US**. I served for US. I am still united to defend **US** against all enemies, foreign and domestic but the **US** within all of **US** must unite and grow into loving the intricacies, cultures, and individualities throughout all of **US** or there will be a few of our **US** politician's political posturing for self-righteousness, greed, power, and ruling as a past kingdom. An empowerment that will further separate, dictate, authorize, minimize, and destroy **US**.

Are we still lost, or do we know another way?

Race categories and racism is America's history can't be hidden or overlooked. One race being asked to be righted because of decades of inequalities isn't a political mantra or gambling game. "I call your racism and I raised you with reverse racism." So, did racism and discrimination exist in America's past for there to be reverse racism and anti-affirmative actions to be today? If so, did political fluency and financial advantageous of WHAAATE exist in America's past for reverse finacial and reparations to be afforded to non-whites today? How empathetic are we toward past and current generations of non-whites being stereotyped, absent, and discriminated against in all facets of life through radio, television, movies, books, and marginalized in educational curriculums as only being a slave or laborer in America's structure, existent, and freedom.

This is for the RIGHT. The right-side of humanity. Be better, ready, and mentally prepared for those interactions with racists who don't know why your skin-tone alone is causing their hate; they are winging it and slinging it in hope something they've been taught sticks. It's most likely nothing they know. Someone out of harm's way is usually the puppeteer controlling and pushing their hate and reaping an agenda (money). It's true, money is a seed and root for evil.

Driving through life, while being mindful that

Woke-up _____ on ____/_____/_____   M   T   W   T   F   S   S   Hours of sleep ____

Sunny__   Cloudy__   Rainy__   Stormy__   Lightning__   Windy__   WTHail__   Snow__   WTMother Nature__

TODAY, I AM

☐	☐	☐	☐	☐	☐	STOP	☐	☐	☐	☐	☐	☐
GREAT	HOPEFUL	AWESOME	MINDFUL	BOLD	ENCOURAGED		GROUCHY	HURT	ANGRY	MAD	BELLIGERENT	ENRAGED
GOOD	HAPPY	ACTIVE	MOTIVATED	BRILLIANT	ENERGIZED		GUARDED	HATEFUL	ANNOYED	MOODY	BITTER	EXHAUSTED

TODAY, I AM GRATEFUL & EXCITED ABOUT:

_____

_____

_____

_____

_____

_____

_____

_____

_____

_____

_____

_____

_____

_____

_____

_____

_____

_____

_____

_____

_____

_____

_____

_____

LAST WORD IN ("Best Moment of Today" – "My Final Thought on Today" – "NOPE!, Never Again"):

$h!+ happeneds

☐ **Another Great Day! A definite and positive day. "I Love Me"**

Driving

Roadside Assistance-How does someone know you need assistance on the side of the road?

- Are you receptive to assistance?
- Is it visible to a passerby if you need assistance?
- Do you care for any passerby's assistance?

through life

Assistance-How does someone know you need help, assistance, comfort, or condolences?

- Do you care if anyone cares, and are you receptive to their attention?
- Is it known or visible to someone you need assistance with?
- Should you expect someone you don't interact with to know if you aren't emotionally or physically the same?

while being mindful

Direct involvement in problematic situations doesn't always require face-to-face or hands-on contact. A phone call for someone in need of assistance is assisting. Watching over from a safe distance until professional help arrives is assisting. Taking mental or written notes to pass on later if needed is assisting.

What's the usual: (Own Kind Against You)
What's not OKAY to believe: (Own Kind Against You)

What's spoken: "They're all against you"
What's never discuss but gains traction or reaction: "My Own Friends Against Me!"

What's whispered: "Your spouse and children are against you"
What's never discuss but gains traction or reaction: "My Own Family Against Me!"

What's gossiped: "Your parents are ashamed and disappointed in you."
What's never discuss but gains traction or reaction: "My Own Parents Turning Against Me!"

What's gossiped: "People are talking"
What's never discuss but gains traction or reaction: "My Own People Against Me!"

What's easier to allow to seep in: "They don't want you on the team."
What's never discuss but gains traction or reaction: "My Own Team Against Me!"

What should be stated or heard: "I had a discussion with…"
What should be the usual: A discussion for asking, understanding, and discovering the truth. Never rely on assumptions, hearsay, gossip, or purposeful lies to be the facts and cause unnecessary discord, dissociation, or divorce. Most importantly, talk it over to confirm.

Driving through life, while being mindful that

Woke-up _____ on ____/_____/_____   M T W T F S S   Hours of sleep ____

Sunny__ Cloudy__ Rainy__ Stormy__ Lightning__ Windy__ WTHail__ Snow__ WTMother Nature__

TODAY, I AM

☐ ☐ ☐ ☐ ☐ ☐ 🛑 ☐ ☐ ☐ ☐ ☐ ☐

| GREAT | HOPEFUL | AWESOME | MINDFUL | BOLD | ENCOURAGED | | GROUCHY | HURT | ANGRY | MAD | BELLIGERENT | ENRAGED |
| GOOD | HAPPY | ACTIVE | MOTIVATED | BRILLIANT | ENERGIZED | | GUARDED | HATEFUL | ANNOYED | MOODY | BITTER | EXHAUSTED |

TODAY, I AM GRATEFUL & EXCITED ABOUT:

_____

_____
_____
_____
_____
_____
_____
_____
_____
_____
_____
_____
_____
_____
_____
_____
_____
_____
_____
_____
_____
_____
_____
_____

LAST WORD IN ("Best Moment of Today" – "My Final Thought on Today" – "NOPE!, Never Again"):

$h!+ happeneds

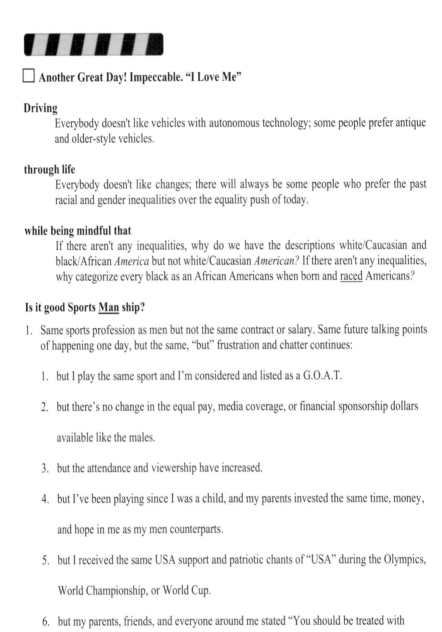

☐ **Another Great Day! Impeccable. "I Love Me"**

Driving

Everybody doesn't like vehicles with autonomous technology; some people prefer antique and older-style vehicles.

through life

Everybody doesn't like changes; there will always be some people who prefer the past racial and gender inequalities over the equality push of today.

while being mindful that

If there aren't any inequalities, why do we have the descriptions white/Caucasian and black/African *America* but not white/Caucasian *American?* If there aren't any inequalities, why categorize every black as an African Americans when born and <u>raced</u> Americans?

Is it good Sports <u>Man</u> ship?

1. Same sports profession as men but not the same contract or salary. Same future talking points of happening one day, but the same, "but" frustration and chatter continues:

    1. but I play the same sport and I'm considered and listed as a G.O.A.T.

    2. but there's no change in the equal pay, media coverage, or financial sponsorship dollars available like the males.

    3. but the attendance and viewership have increased.

    4. but I've been playing since I was a child, and my parents invested the same time, money, and hope in me as my men counterparts.

    5. but I received the same USA support and patriotic chants of "USA" during the Olympics, World Championship, or World Cup.

    6. but my parents, friends, and everyone around me stated "You should be treated with dignity and respect" and "You should expect to be treated with dignity and respect."

    7. but it will happen one day as woman suffrage changed in 1920/1965 (backward in 2022).

    8. but _____.

    <u>Sports Man</u> ship: lets debate & distract from money inequality by angering w/transgenders.

Woke-up _____ on _____/_____/_____   M T W T F S S   Hours of sleep ____

Sunny__ Cloudy__ Rainy__ Stormy__ Lightning__ Windy__ WTHail__ Snow__ WTMother Nature__

TODAY, I AM

☐ | ☐ | ☐ | ☐ | ☐ | ☐ | STOP | ☐ | ☐ | ☐ | ☐ | ☐ | ☐

| GREAT | HOPEFUL | AWESOME | MINDFUL | BOLD | ENCOURAGED | | GROUCHY | HURT | ANGRY | MAD | BELLIGERENT | ENRAGED |
| GOOD | HAPPY | ACTIVE | MOTIVATED | BRILLIANT | ENERGIZED | | GUARDED | HATEFUL | ANNOYED | MOODY | BITTER | EXHAUSTED |

TODAY, I AM GRATEFUL & EXCITED ABOUT:

_____

_____

_____

_____

_____

_____

_____

_____

_____

_____

_____

_____

_____

_____

_____

_____

_____

_____

_____

_____

_____

_____

_____

_____

LAST WORD IN ("Best Moment of Today" – "My Final Thought on Today" – "NOPE!, Never Again"):

$h!+ happeneds

☐ **Another Great Day! Fight the Power & Fight for the Powerless. "I Love Me"**

Driving

If there's a road sign with "Road Closed," "Do not enter," or "Only for residence," but the road is not visibly blocked or manned by anyone; do you enter?

through life

If there are no cameras or anyone to witness you doing something wrong, illegal, or immoral, do you do the wrong?

while being mindful

Save the youths. May the youth be with us.

Our youth's rights to vote are under attack. We must afford the next generation their right to vote and the right for those votes to be counted. Do not forget the political democracy debacle and world embarrassment that happened at our United States Capital. We must remind ourselves that Trusting Racist Unethical Minded People and Trusting Resurrectionist Under Minding Politicians is a DANGER to our DEMOCRACY, NATION, and FUTURE. America, what do you got to lose by trusting wrong? Rights or Democracy

- Whites don't be outfoxed or overpowered by WHAAATES or IHAAATE People.
- BLACK PEOPLE don't be duped by historical books written, published, and distributed by individuals that weren't BLACK and weren't empowered to empower BLACKS through literature. A History of Managing, Mandates, Manipulation, & Mansplaining
- PROUD PATRIOTS don't be bamboozled by a POLITICIAN'S PROFITTING PROPAGANDA. POLITICIANS stop being deceived and appeased by DONATIONS
- MAGA constituents don't be conned by fearmongering and opportunists who are really MAKING AMERICA GHASTLY AGAIN.
- YOUTH don't be hoodwinked by the well-oiled and grease economical hate fueling and dividing system of elitism and politicians and their WHAAATE donor minions.
- PARENTS & GUARDIANS don't allow your daughters to be victimized by misogynist men for being a WOMAN or any of your children for being happy for who they are. https://www.amnesty.org/en/what-we-do/discrimination/womens-rights/
- All other non-whites don't be misled by the NEWS that's created, directed, and aired for or by dollars (political discord and race hate illumination feeds the media machine).

Why you should have trust issue when it comes to any politician joking about democracy?
Dictatorship Exhibit A: Look at the Authoritarianism of other nations on display America.

1. *Deport or lock them up. "No American can speak again our ~~Administration~~ Regime."*
2. *One-sided fake news/media forever "We control social media input, output and specified outages"*
3. *~~"We the People"~~ "We the One's in Power" "It's one party/religion rule going forward"*
4. *No checks and balance. "I am your ~~leader~~ ruler and I deserve my opulent lifestyle" It's a law now*
5. *"America's specified ~~businesses~~ oligarchs' partners will receive all government contract"*
6. *"I/We knows what's best for the nation" "We feel the U.S Constitution needs amending"*
7. *"Yes, my family/political party member will succeed my ~~presidency~~ corruption" It's a Law*
8. *"We will decide who can participate in our voting process" It's a Law*
9. *No office transparency (already in use). Schools: Every child is indoctrinated to follow one system.*
10. *Women's Exhibit A: Afghan women (no voice or choice). But no, not America."2022" next B&P?*

Driving through life, while being mindful that

Woke-up _____ on ____/____/____   M T W T F S S   Hours of sleep ____

Sunny__ Cloudy__ Rainy__ Stormy__ Lightning__ Windy__ WTHail__ Snow__ WTMother Nature__

TODAY, I AM

☐	☐	☐	☐	☐	☐	🛑 STOP	☐	☐	☐	☐	☐	☐
GREAT	HOPEFUL	AWESOME	MINDFUL	BOLD	ENCOURAGED		GROUCHY	HURT	ANGRY	MAD	BELLIGERENT	ENRAGED
GOOD	HAPPY	ACTIVE	MOTIVATED	BRILLIANT	ENERGIZED		GUARDED	HATEFUL	ANNOYED	MOODY	BITTER	EXHAUSTED

TODAY, I AM GRATEFUL & EXCITED ABOUT:

_____

_____
_____
_____
_____
_____
_____
_____
_____
_____
_____
_____
_____
_____
_____
_____
_____
_____
_____
_____
_____
_____
_____
_____
_____

LAST WORD IN ("Best Moment of Today" – "My Final Thought on Today" – "NOPE!, Never Again"):

$h!+ happeneds

☐ **Another Great Day! Optimizing at its finest. "I Love Me"**

Driving

There are no alcoholic beverages designed or explicitly prescribed for driving, so deciding to put any alcohol-influencing substance in your systems before operating a vehicle is your poor decision.

through life

Life and death decisions aren't just made by doctors.

- Do you know the success rate of those who consider not too much versus those whose organs realize it was too much alcohol or drugs?
- Do you choose to eat unhealthy food daily to support the pharmaceutical and healthcare business?
- Does buying the cheapest foods with insufficient nutrients save you enough money to pay for your high medical costs from eating wrong or too much?
- Should you be concerned about missing one day of work for a medical appointment, treatment, checkup, therapy, or do you prefer being admitted and missing several days or weeks from work for not going?
- Who gains if you do right in your life, and who suffers if you don't change?
- Did answering any of the above questions give you any appreciation for a doctor deciding your life or death, or did it make you appreciate you having that decision first?

while being mindful

Funerals are life reminders:

- It reminds the living that sickness and hospitalization is serious.
- It reminds the living that each breath of life is extraordinary.
- It reminds the living that death pains those left behind.
- It reminds the living to appreciate simplicity and complicatedness the same.
- It reminds the living that no one lives forever.
- It reminds the living that racism, religious righteous, and hate ideology kills.
- It reminds the living that race, status, or wealth doesn't prevent death.
- It reminds the living that each kiss, hug, touch, and laugh is profoundly special.
- It reminds the living the loss of life can happen at any moment.
- It reminds the living to appreciate and remain humble.
- It reminds the living that you're categorized at birth, but death sorts us all the same.

Empathetic Pauses

Always try to be understanding, courteous, and respectful to those suffering a loss of life. Be courteous and yield to all funeral processions; when possible, pull over and give the vehicles in the procession their right of way.

Woke-up _____ on _____/_____/_____ M T W T F S S   Hours of sleep ____

Sunny__ Cloudy__ Rainy__ Stormy__ Lightning__ Windy__ WTHail__ Snow__ WTMother Nature__

TODODAY, I AM

GREAT	HOPEFUL	AWESOME	MINDFUL	BOLD	ENCOURAGED	STOP	GROUCHY	HURT	ANGRY	MAD	BELLIGERENT	ENRAGED
GOOD	HAPPY	ACTIVE	MOTIVATED	BRILLIANT	ENERGIZED		GUARDED	HATEFUL	ANNOYED	MOODY	BITTER	EXHAUSTED

TODAY, I AM GRATEFUL & EXCITED ABOUT:

_____

_____

_____

_____

_____

_____

_____

_____

_____

_____

_____

_____

_____

_____

_____

_____

_____

_____

_____

_____

_____

_____

_____

LAST WORD IN ("Best Moment of Today" – "My Final Thought on Today" – "NOPE!, Never Again"):

$h!+ happeneds

☐ **Another Great Day! Game on. "I Love Me"**

Driving

If a white vehicle strikes a black vehicle, white paint will be transferred onto the black vehicle. If a black vehicle strikes a white vehicle, there will be black paint transferred onto the white vehicle.

through life

Racism and hate toward anyone are wrong. Being in the presence of racism and hate tarnishes every person's energy present.

while being mindful

Choose to teach, preach, or outreach with love because choosing to hate continues the hate.

Permanent Tattoo Pain vs Racism & Discrimination Pain

Is getting a tattoo hurtful?

Tattoo Artist: It doesn't hurt that much.
Canvas #1. Yes, it hurts.
Canvas #2. It depends on who and how it's done.
Canvas #3. Sometimes. I try not to focus on it when it's done.
Canvas #4. You will know when it happens to you.
Canvas #5. Very Painful

Is racism and discrimination hurtful?

Racist/Bigot#1. It's my right to say (1st A) or be...
Victim #1. Yes, it hurts.
Victim #2. It depends on who and how it's done (context, communication, or culpability).
Victim #3. Sometimes. I try not to focus on it when it's done. (it doesn't bother me, really)
Victim #4. You will know when it happens to you.
Victim #5. It's Very Painful (Physically, Financially, Finacially, Mentally, Socially, & Spiritually)

Math word problem (difficulties varies)
Basic Math-Race
Algebra-Racism
Trigonometry-Racist

*Education, empathy, and experienced educators helps (where allowed and not illegal or politicized)

***Can you define conserve?**

Driving through life, while being mindful that

Woke-up _____ on ____/____/____ M T W T F S S   Hours of sleep ____

Sunny__ Cloudy__ Rainy__ Stormy__ Lightning__ Windy__ WTHail__ Snow__ WTMother Nature__

TODAY, I AM

☐	☐	☐	☐	☐	☐	STOP	☐	☐	☐	☐	☐	☐
GREAT	HOPEFUL	AWESOME	MINDFUL	BOLD	ENCOURAGED		GROUCHY	HURT	ANGRY	MAD	BELLIGERENT	ENRAGED
GOOD	HAPPY	ACTIVE	MOTIVATED	BRILLIANT	ENERGIZED		GUARDED	HATEFUL	ANNOYED	MOODY	BITTER	EXHAUSTED

TODAY, I AM GRATEFUL & EXCITED ABOUT:

_____

_____

_____

_____

_____

_____

_____

_____

_____

_____

_____

_____

_____

_____

_____

_____

_____

_____

_____

_____

_____

_____

_____

LAST WORD IN ("Best Moment of Today" – "My Final Thought on Today" – "NOPE!, Never Again"):

$h!+ happeneds

☐ **Another Great Day! It's a part of me now. I got this. "I Love Me"**

Driving

What would you do if your borrowed vehicle was carelessly damaged again by the same person who borrowed and damaged it last time?

- Do you forgive, forget, or excuse yourself?
- Do you tell the driver they're in a probationary period and must take a driver's training course?
- Do you give one more opportunity, or was the last damage their final time driving?

through life

What would you do if your loving heart was carelessly hurt in a relationship by the same person again?

- Do you forgive, forget, or excuse yourself?
- Do you tell the person they must seek professional help and counseling before continuing?
- Do you give them one more chance to heal or was the first hurt enough pain?

while being mindful

Reminder: The heart is as vulnerable inside as outside. If your heart was on the outside of your body, would you allow anyone to come up and grab it, squeeze it, inject something toxic, or throw something on it?

Woke-up _____ on _____/_____/_____   M T W T F S S   Hours of sleep _____

Sunny__ Cloudy__ Rainy__ Stormy__ Lightning__ Windy__ WTHail__ Snow__ WTMother Nature__

TODAY, I AM

☐	☐	☐	☐	☐	☐	STOP	☐	☐	☐	☐	☐	☐
GREAT	HOPEFUL	AWESOME	MINDFUL	BOLD	ENCOURAGED		GROUCHY	HURT	ANGRY	MAD	BELLIGERENT	ENRAGED
GOOD	HAPPY	ACTIVE	MOTIVATED	BRILLIANT	ENERGIZED		GUARDED	HATEFUL	ANNOYED	MOODY	BITTER	EXHAUSTED

TODAY, I AM GRATEFUL & EXCITED ABOUT:

_____
_____
_____
_____
_____
_____
_____
_____
_____
_____
_____
_____
_____
_____
_____
_____
_____
_____
_____
_____
_____
_____
_____
_____

LAST WORD IN ("Best Moment of Today" – "My Final Thought on Today" – "NOPE!, Never Again"):

$h!+ happeneds

☐ **Another Great Day! Be committed. "I Love Me"**

Driving
- What should you do if you fail to pass the vision exam required to obtain a driver's license?
- What should you do if you fail to pass the knowledge test required to obtain a license?
- What should you do if you fail to pass the road test required to obtain a driver's license?
- What should you do if your license is suspended or revoked?
- What should you do if your license expires?

through life
- What should you do if you make a mistake?
- What happens if you make another mistake?
- What should you do if you fail to accomplish any task or goal?
- What happens if you make another mistake after being released from incarceration or rehabilitation?
- What should you do if you notice your life is spiraling out of control with health and finances?

while being mindful
   BE COMMITTED.
   1. Fail & Failing is still better than Failed & Failure.
   2. Fail, Failing, Failed, or Failure are word motivators because each one be ascended higher or changed to represent a better future.
   3. Yesterday was the past you, but today is the present you. Today, I'm better today, I'm moving forward today, I'm reaching out for help today. Today,
      ☐ I won't make any excuses.
      ☐ I slipped a little but tomorrow…
      ☐ I finally realized…
      ☐ I invested in my future.
      ☐ I changed. I moved on.
      ☐ I know I deserve better for me.
      ☐ I reported it.
      ☐ I listened to my inner strength.
      ☐ I am better. I overcame it. I am here.
      ☐ I spoke up. I was seen and I was heard.
      ☐ I succeeded yesterday and my yesteryear.
      ☐ I am wiser and I will try again.
      ☐ I will seek the truth that's being hidden, banned, and politicized.
      ☐ I will stand with and against…
      ☐ I march, protest, boycott, speak up, petition, unionize, ask questions, or vote.
      ☐ I will applaud, recognize, thank, recommend, or praise someone's greatness.
      ☐ I am blessed, empowered, favored, overjoyed, and thankful for another day.

      Today, I _____.

Driving through life, while being mindful that

Woke-up _____ on ____/____/____   M T W T F S S   Hours of sleep ____

Sunny__ Cloudy__ Rainy__ Stormy__ Lightning__ Windy__ WTHail__ Snow__ WTMother Nature__

TODAY, I AM

☐	☐	☐	☐	☐	☐		☐	☐	☐	☐	☐	☐
GREAT	HOPEFUL	AWESOME	MINDFUL	BOLD	ENCOURAGED	STOP	GROUCHY	HURT	ANGRY	MAD	BELLIGERENT	ENRAGED
GOOD	HAPPY	ACTIVE	MOTIVATED	BRILLIANT	ENERGIZED		GUARDED	HATEFUL	ANNOYED	MOODY	BITTER	EXHAUSTED

TODAY, I AM GRATEFUL & EXCITED ABOUT:

_____

_____

_____

_____

_____

_____

_____

_____

_____

_____

_____

_____

_____

_____

_____

_____

_____

_____

_____

_____

_____

_____

_____

_____

_____

LAST WORD IN ("Best Moment of Today" – "My Final Thought on Today" – "NOPE!, Never Again"):

$h!+ happeneds

☐ **Another Great Day! Not guaranteed for everyone today. "I Love Me"**

Driving

> Most cars need the bare necessities to function (air, water, oil, and gas). Make maintaining your vehicle simple and inexpensive by disregarding every marketed high-performing supplement or solvent.

through life

> Most people need the bare necessities to function (air, food, water, rest, shelter, clothing, and some interaction of one or few).

while being mindful

> "Hey, People?" You can organize your life much better by categorizing who needs to be in your life temporarily vs. permanently. All your friends and family members shouldn't be categorized as best, close, or permanent; some are temporary and will only be associated by name, family gathering, borrowing/owing, favor(s), money, fame association, or through social media interaction only.

WTFYS – What's the fraction you solved?

Would you appreciate someone referring to you as their best friend but only texting you once or twice a year without ever calling or attempting to meet up? Should your friend expect the same if you're in dereliction of the same communication or meeting efforts?

FT GHAMBE

Woke-up _____ on ____/____/____ M T W T F S S   Hours of sleep ____

Sunny__ Cloudy__ Rainy__ Stormy__ Lightning__ Windy__ WTHail__ Snow__ WTMother Nature__

TODAY, I AM

☐ GREAT / GOOD
☐ HOPEFUL / HAPPY
☐ AWESOME / ACTIVE
☐ MINDFUL / MOTIVATED
☐ BOLD / BRILLIANT
☐ ENCOURAGED / ENERGIZED

STOP

☐ GROUCHY / GUARDED
☐ HURT / HATEFUL
☐ ANGRY / ANNOYED
☐ MAD / MOODY
☐ BELLIGERENT / BITTER
☐ ENRAGED / EXHAUSTED

TODAY, I AM GRATEFUL & EXCITED ABOUT:

_____
_____
_____
_____
_____
_____
_____
_____
_____
_____
_____
_____
_____
_____
_____
_____
_____
_____
_____
_____
_____

LAST WORD IN ("Best Moment of Today" – "My Final Thought on Today" – "NOPE!, Never Again"):

$h!+ happeneds

☐ **Another Great Day! Engaging. "I Love Me"**

Driving

You should know the legal age to drive before you start practicing driving.

through life

Do you know the legal age for sex where you're residing or are you having sex without verification or of age legal clarity? Adult, if this prompt is below you, it may be well above a teenager or young adult family member' mental awareness close to you.

- First, you must know your state's penal code age to consent to sex.
- Secondly, you must know their parents' or legal guardians' consenting age for sex.
- Third and Final: You must not have any doubt about age and consent.
- **Summary:** DO NOT wait to find out the legal age of those who consented to have sex with you during police questioning, face-face with their parent, or in court awaiting all to rise command.

while being mindful

It is never good for the court to tell you something you should know. A defendant will follow a lawyer's advice on how their actions, demeanor, and style of dressing should be for court but won't listen to anyone significant, close, and loving advising the same before doing wrong. It's best to learn about being humble about life before being instructed on how to be humbled before appearing before a judge.

In law enforcement interaction, what is an officer's "PC"?
a) Personal Concern
b) Probable Cause
c) Planned Concoction
d) Personal Courage
e) Personal Choice
f) Privilege Communication

In family member's interaction or intervention for an abusive relations, alcohol, or drug addiction; what is your "PC"?
a) Personal Concern
b) Probable Cause
c) Planned Concoction
d) Personal Courage
e) Personal Choice
f) Privilege Communication

*To be an intricate part of any intervention, you must wholeheartedly believe in People's Care.

Woke-up _____ on _____/_____/_____   M T W T F S S   Hours of sleep ____

Sunny__ Cloudy__ Rainy__ Stormy__   Lightning__ Windy__ WTHail__ Snow__ WTMother Nature__

TODAY, I AM

☐	☐	☐	☐	☐	☐	🛑	☐	☐	☐	☐	☐	☐
GREAT	HOPEFUL	AWESOME	MINDFUL	BOLD	ENCOURAGED	STOP	GROUCHY	HURT	ANGRY	MAD	BELLIGERENT	ENRAGED
GOOD	HAPPY	ACTIVE	MOTIVATED	BRILLIANT	ENERGIZED		GUARDED	HATEFUL	ANNOYED	MOODY	BITTER	EXHAUSTED

TODAY, I AM GRATEFUL & EXCITED ABOUT:

_____

_____

_____

_____

_____

_____

_____

_____

_____

_____

_____

_____

_____

_____

_____

_____

_____

_____

_____

_____

_____

_____

_____

_____

_____

LAST WORD IN ("Best Moment of Today" – "My Final Thought on Today" – "NOPE!, Never Again"):

$h!+ happeneds

☐ **Another Great Day! BINGO! "I Love Me"**

Driving

>Nobody means to cause a vehicle accident, but accidents with damage and injuries still occur. If you're involved in an accident collision with others, always assume unknown injuries and always try to send emergency help as soon as possible.

through life

>Using "I didn't mean to" doesn't make what was done go away. If you're involved in an altercation with someone, always assume attitudes could escalate before it's safe. Always try to de-escalate any aggression or hostility; if not, remain silent, walk away, and remove yourself from the threat. If a law or right has been violated (communicating threat, assault, or property damage) and if not in danger, please await the arrival of emergency service or law professionals to make sure your side is heard.

while being mindful

>Venting never cools down or warms the individual feeling your airiness. Voicing your concern toward the person you're in a disagreement with about their customer servicing is usually not the best option. It's okay to disagree with a person, policy, product, or service of an establishment but make sure you voice your concern to the person who has the authority to make a difference in what you disagree with instead of those who don't.

It's no longer a personal or internal matter.

Hearing "After the fact" comment is usually not good.

Woke-up _____ on ____/____/____   M T W T F S S   Hours of sleep ____

Sunny__ Cloudy__ Rainy__ Stormy__ Lightning__ Windy__ WTHail__ Snow__ WTMother Nature__

TODAY, I AM

☐ GREAT ☐ HOPEFUL ☐ AWESOME ☐ MINDFUL ☐ BOLD ☐ ENCOURAGED **STOP** ☐ GROUCHY ☐ HURT ☐ ANGRY ☐ MAD ☐ BELLIGERENT ☐ ENRAGED

GOOD   HAPPY   ACTIVE   MOTIVATED   BRILLIANT   ENERGIZED   GUARDED   HATEFUL   ANNOYED   MOODY   BITTER   EXHAUSTED

TODAY, I AM GRATEFUL & EXCITED ABOUT:

_____

_____

_____

_____

_____

_____

_____

_____

_____

_____

_____

_____

_____

_____

_____

_____

_____

_____

_____

_____

_____

_____

_____

_____

LAST WORD IN ("Best Moment of Today" – "My Final Thought on Today" – "NOPE!, Never Again"):

$h!+ happeneds

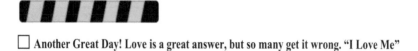

☐ **Another Great Day! Love is a great answer, but so many get it wrong. "I Love Me"**

Driving

Make sure you have vehicle insurance coverage, and the proof of coverage is present in the vehicle digitally or by insurance card before operating.

through life

Make sure you have some insurance coverage for yourself (life, medical, home, and death) before it's a burden on your family.

while being mindful

Financial discussions, understanding, or agreements (prenup) before traditional or commonwealth marriages aren't only for the wealthy. Choose what's best for y<u>our</u> peace of mind or mitigation. Your state laws may vary.

Our Love, Marriage, and Forever Togetherness.

1. In relationships, it's what yours is yours.

2. In marriage, it's what y**ours** is y̶**Ours**

3. In divorce, it's what was y̶**Ours** is Y̶**OURS**

state laws will vary

Woke-up _____ on ____/____/____ M T W T F S S   Hours of sleep ____

Sunny__ Cloudy__ Rainy__ Stormy__ Lightning__ Windy__ WTHail__ Snow__ WTMother Nature__

TODAY, I AM

☐ ☐ ☐ ☐ ☐ ☐ **STOP** ☐ ☐ ☐ ☐ ☐ ☐

GREAT HOPEFUL AWESOME MINDFUL BOLD ENCOURAGED | GROUCHY HURT ANGRY MAD BELLIGERENT ENRAGED

GOOD HAPPY ACTIVE MOTIVATED BRILLIANT ENERGIZED | GUARDED HATEFUL ANNOYED MOODY BITTER EXHAUSTED

TODAY, I AM GRATEFUL & EXCITED ABOUT:

_____
_____
_____
_____
_____
_____
_____
_____
_____
_____
_____
_____
_____
_____
_____
_____
_____
_____
_____
_____
_____
_____

LAST WORD IN ("Best Moment of Today" – "My Final Thought on Today" – "NOPE!, Never Again"):

$h!+ happeneds

☐ **Another Great Day! No palm reading was required. "I Love Me"**

Driving

> **What does the color of the vehicle have to do with its performance or durability?**
> Will a black car go faster than a white car?
> Will a black car go further than the white car? Or Vice versa
> Will a black car break down before the white car?

through life

> Racism WTF?

- What's the Fault? systematic racism, desperation, privilege, and fear mongering.
- What's the Failure? never recognizing and still not recognizing the updated truthfulness of the past. Still milking the slave lesser than instead of glorifying and championing the United States being established, developed, constructed, united, and saved by lives sacrificed in wars by all.
- Where's the Faithful? Where's the outrage of the faithful for all Gods people?
- What's the Future? Admission, infrastructure reparation and racial classification deconstruction.
- Where's the Foolishness? Racist and racism still being relevant and prevalent today.
- What's the Facts (a few of many)?
  1. Slavery, Jim Crow, Equal rights must be <u>granted</u> citizens (blacks & women)
  2. Special Field Orders No. 15
  3. Indian reservations would always belong to the tribes.
  4. Broken Indian treaties agreement?
  5. The Indian Removal Act
  6. History of the dethroning Kingdoms & Tribes (African/Hawaiian/Native Americans) and taking land ownership. Festive or Jealous of the remaining Kingdom.
  7. Skin color determines an individual's threat before investigation, witness, weapon visibility, or threat is known or displayed.
  8. For America to succeed as one and be united, citizens must still pick a political side, gender, religion, or skin tone shade of color.
  9. Who's controlling the educational histories and truths of Africans, Indians, and Hawaiians? Who owns the most land or cultural centers (Luas) of the cultures?

while being mindful that all knowledge (proven and disproven) strengthens knowledge.

- The Power of an Illusion by PBS.org **or** Historical Foundations of Race by NMAAHC
- La Hoihoi Ea https://lahoihoiea.org/ How was the Kingdom of Hawaii was overthrown?
- Native Americans https://americanindian.si.edu/nk360/faq/did-you-know
- Women's Rights https://www.amnesty.org/en/what-we-do/discrimination/womens-rights/
- National Museum of African American https://www.si.edu/museums/african-american-museum

Disclaimer: The sites are used solely for information.

Woke-up _____ on ____/_____/_____   M T W T F S S   Hours of sleep ____

Sunny__ Cloudy__ Rainy__ Stormy__ Lightning__ Windy__ WTHail__ Snow__ WTMother Nature__

TODAY, I AM

☐	☐	☐	☐	☐	☐	**STOP**	☐	☐	☐	☐	☐	☐
GREAT	HOPEFUL	AWESOME	MINDFUL	BOLD	ENCOURAGED		GROUCHY	HURT	ANGRY	MAD	BELLIGERENT	ENRAGED
GOOD	HAPPY	ACTIVE	MOTIVATED	BRILLIANT	ENERGIZED		GUARDED	HATEFUL	ANNOYED	MOODY	BITTER	EXHAUSTED

TODAY, I AM GRATEFUL & EXCITED ABOUT:

_____

_____
_____
_____
_____
_____
_____
_____
_____
_____
_____
_____
_____
_____
_____
_____
_____
_____
_____
_____
_____
_____
_____
_____

LAST WORD IN ("Best Moment of Today" – "My Final Thought on Today" – "NOPE!, Never Again"):

$h!+ happeneds

☐ **Another Great Day! Don't stop. Keep smiling. "I Love Me"**

Driving

Every drive is different. You will encounter different traffic each day and every drive will cause more wear and tear on the vehicle's body and engine.

through life

Every day is different. You will encounter different individuals with varied moods each day and every day your body will act a little differently, react a little differently, and be different thereafter.

while being mindful

Live, Learn, Lounge, Laugh, Listen, Lead, and Love. A lot of action words, but each day, you will have an opportunity to accomplish them all in one day, with one always being automatic. ***an exception to the above rule is an abusive relationship. A lot of actions words, but each day the abuse is hopeful for one, with one being required but never guaranteed. National Domestic Violence Hotline (Speak with someone today) 800-799-7233 Hours: 24/7. Languages: English, Spanish and 200+ through interpretation service SMS: Text START to 88788 National Teen Dating Abuse Helpline The Helpline's peer advocates serve thousands of teens and young adults through the 24/7 phone service. Users call 1-866-331-9474 to be connected with an advocate who is trained to offer education, support and advocacy to those involved in dating abuse relationships as well as concerned friends, siblings, parents, teachers, law enforcement members and service providers.**

Woke-up _____ on ____/____/____   M T W T F S S   Hours of sleep ____

Sunny__ Cloudy__ Rainy__ Stormy__ Lightning__ Windy__ WTHail__ Snow__ WTMother Nature__

TODAY, I AM

☐	☐	☐	☐	☐	☐	STOP	☐	☐	☐	☐	☐	☐
GREAT	HOPEFUL	AWESOME	MINDFUL	BOLD	ENCOURAGED		GROUCHY	HURT	ANGRY	MAD	BELLIGERENT	ENRAGED
GOOD	HAPPY	ACTIVE	MOTIVATED	BRILLIANT	ENERGIZED		GUARDED	HATEFUL	ANNOYED	MOODY	BITTER	EXHAUSTED

TODAY, I AM GRATEFUL & EXCITED ABOUT:

_____

_____

_____

_____

_____

_____

_____

_____

_____

_____

_____

_____

_____

_____

_____

_____

_____

_____

_____

_____

_____

_____

_____

LAST WORD IN ("Best Moment of Today" – "My Final Thought on Today" – "NOPE!, Never Again"):

$h!+ happeneds

☐ **Another Great Day! Respect. "I Love Me"**

Driving
> Parking: Never leave a child or animals in hot or freezing cold vehicles.

through life
> Any living species left alone in an extremely hot or cold enclosure can lead to death.

while being mindful
> You rarely hear a politician state "What I am going to tell you is a lie or truth."
> An illusion of a magic trick is what the magician tells you to focus on (something going to disappear) instead of what leads to the illusion. The illusion of a financial con is to have you focus on the highly transparent number they once received (possibly) but not as transparent as your current stock portfolio numbers. The illusion of a politician is to have you focused on what they say instead of what they supposed to do (vote, sign, or pass laws for all citizens "We the People"; not WHAAATE People or IHAAATE People.

1. Why does inflation or bankruptcy filing cause the owners and executive salaries or their exit packages to increase but not the employees?
2. Why are their parents voicing their concerns over books but silent safety, security, or about food malnutrition and malnourishment in schools?
3. It's difficult for politicians to come to a bipartisan government agreement to connect American constituents but easy for them to come to agreement with a far left or far right group for an agreement on donations and votes.
4. Why are politicians so concern over pharmaceutical's birth control drugs but no control or wherewithal toward pharmaceutical companies pushing drug destroying communities and ending lives (babies included).

Have you asked the family or your chosen political party (only two to choose from) when is the United States demolition date schedule?
America's race and political structure in human relations to other nations around the world is like witnessing a stable and sound structure being demolished around other stable structures. Americans of late, are hiring (electing) the most hateful, racist, and zaniest politician (speaks craziness as I think) to demolish America. As America continues to place the race and economic divide explosive for a perfect detonation to implode inward on itself as planned by "so called" chosen few, the only structures left standing tall will be the other nations. While the others nation's structure thrives and move upward, we; the Americans will still be infighting over who's more American, skin-tones, cultures, books, fair wage, non-taxed trillionaires, and America's medical and educational money juggernaut with payments that mirrors or bypass home mortgages. Busy voicing displeasure of other nation's government leaders and politicians being authoritarian and corrupted, while allowing the same. Busy voicing rights outrage about government not being transparent but allowing tax paid political representatives to shield their government funded movements and meetings with who knows who or about what's planned.

<u>**Big Questions**</u>. Who will suffer? **us** Who will oversee the democracy detonation? **Not us but US**

Woke-up _____ on _____/_____/_____   M T W T F S S   Hours of sleep _____

Sunny__ Cloudy__ Rainy__ Stormy__ Lightning__ Windy__ WTHail__ Snow__ WTMother Nature__

TODAY, I AM

☐	☐	☐	☐	☐	☐	STOP	☐	☐	☐	☐	☐	☐
GREAT	HOPEFUL	AWESOME	MINDFUL	BOLD	ENCOURAGED		GROUCHY	HURT	ANGRY	MAD	BELLIGERENT	ENRAGED
GOOD	HAPPY	ACTIVE	MOTIVATED	BRILLIANT	ENERGIZED		GUARDED	HATEFUL	ANNOYED	MOODY	BITTER	EXHAUSTED

TODAY, I AM GRATEFUL & EXCITED ABOUT:

_____

_____

_____

_____

_____

_____

_____

_____

_____

_____

_____

_____

_____

_____

_____

_____

_____

_____

_____

_____

_____

_____

_____

LAST WORD IN ("Best Moment of Today" – "My Final Thought on Today" – "NOPE!, Never Again"):

$h!+ happeneds

☐ **Another Great Day! A democracy allows you to be who you want to be. A dictatorship allows you to be who they want you to be. "I Love Me"**

A few politicians behind closed doors discussing an authoritarian ~~government~~ regime.

1. **Racism-** Why not, every nation treats their blacks, or darker skinned as lesser.
2. **Internet & News Media Control-** Why not, other dictators and authoritarians' control their news narrative and what is shared and allowed online.
3. **Education-** The discord and anger of curriculums will elevate our idea of a Charter / Privatization Biz Model. Also, it's getting difficult to control and manipulate the educated ones.
4. **Financial-** Why not, we must keep all race from being seen or believe as equal. Race/Competing
5. **Minimum wage-** Why increase, we must keep some without to service those of us that are better than.
6. **One Political Party Control-** Why not, two is competition but one-party making laws rules forever.
7. **One Religion-** Why not, it's easier to manipulate and remove citizens' rights as other nations.
1. **Pro-Life-** we will continue to push Pro-Life until that child is born and their parents need help. Also, Pro-Life means more individuals to be taxed, ruled, and be of servitude. Pro-Death/Execution okay.
8. **1st Amendment-** We will continue to voice and champion citizen's rights until we gain control; then we will stop protest, deport and lock-up as a dictatorship.
9. **Penal, Prisons & Probation Conglomerate-** Even though incarceration is rehabilitation, we will still hold their criminality against them to limit their voting rights, career advancement, and the ability to do what is legal now (marijuana industry). Also, crime is one our economy pillars.
10. **Healthcare-** We can still allow certain ingredients. We must limit or remove the use of "process food" to assist the fake/alternative food future. Healthcare is one of our biggest economy pillars.
11. **Immigration-** Continue to campaign "Wall" but ~~allow~~ slip a few undocumented laborers.
12. **Voting Laws-** Must be sustained or alter to remain in power. <u>More Focus</u>: We must limit the young and old voters. Our sports and entertainment minions will confuse the others. The remaining are tired and don't trust or care for voting anymore.
13. We will breakup and re-distribute the government jobs, departments, and entities to civilian sector (American Oligarchs, Associates, Family Members, or whomever we choose) *Ditto for Veteran Affair.*
14. **Fear (continue to perfect fearmongering):**
    Heighten fear> I/we save them from what we informed them to be fearful of > Money is raised, transferred, or allocated by our Bill w/o distribution transparency > We create and establish an entity (associates) to oversee, study, publish new poll (cha-ching)> Our new media partners reverberate the fear rhetoric> Constituents believe and become fearful and Voila', Millions and Billions distributed with few dollars sprinkled to non-profiteers and programs-whatever fear we created to cater or counter.

Woke-up _____ on ____/____/_____ M T W T F S S Hours of sleep ____

Sunny__ Cloudy__ Rainy__ Stormy__ Lightning__ Windy__ WTHail__ Snow__ WTMother Nature__

TODAY, I AM

☐	☐	☐	☐	☐	☐	STOP	☐	☐	☐	☐	☐	☐
GREAT	HOPEFUL	AWESOME	MINDFUL	BOLD	ENCOURAGED		GROUCHY	HURT	ANGRY	MAD	BELLIGERENT	ENRAGED
GOOD	HAPPY	ACTIVE	MOTIVATED	BRILLIANT	ENERGIZED		GUARDED	HATEFUL	ANNOYED	MOODY	BITTER	EXHAUSTED

TODAY, I AM GRATEFUL & EXCITED ABOUT:

_____
_____
_____
_____
_____
_____
_____
_____
_____
_____
_____
_____
_____
_____
_____
_____
_____
_____
_____
_____
_____
_____
_____
_____

LAST WORD IN ("Best Moment of Today" – "My Final Thought on Today" – "NOPE!, Never Again"):

$h!+ happeneds

☐ Stop the presses. Another Great Day! Today, Soak It Up or Soak It In. "I Love Me"

"BREAKING NEWS!"

I interrupt your reading and journaling to bring you this unique piece of peaceful information. Set your mood to "Energetic" or "Great day to be me" today and take a news radio and television news broadcasting day off. <u>Do Not</u> turn on or allow anyone's negative news-producing energy to bombard your day (drive in silence). If riding, ride in your silence (no electronics or phone) and listen to what's going on around you. The silence will assist you in visualizing more and possibly notice someone being missed and overlooked. **Now back to your regular schedule journaling.**

Woke-up _____ on ____/_____/_____   M T W T F S S   Hours of sleep ____

Sunny__ Cloudy__ Rainy__ Stormy__ Lightning__ Windy__ WTHail__ Snow__ WTMother Nature__

TODAY, I AM

☐ ☐ ☐ ☐ ☐ ☐ **STOP** ☐ ☐ ☐ ☐ ☐ ☐

GREAT HOPEFUL AWESOME MINDFUL BOLD ENCOURAGED | GROUCHY HURT ANGRY MAD BELLIGERENT ENRAGED

GOOD HAPPY ACTIVE MOTIVATED BRILLIANT ENERGIZED | GUARDED HATEFUL ANNOYED MOODY BITTER EXHAUSTED

TODAY, I AM GRATEFUL & EXCITED ABOUT:

_____

_____

_____

_____

_____

_____

_____

_____

_____

_____

_____

_____

_____

_____

_____

_____

_____

_____

_____

_____

_____

_____

_____

_____

_____

LAST WORD IN ("Best Moment of Today" – "My Final Thought on Today" – "NOPE!, Never Again"):

$h!+ happeneds

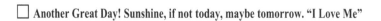

☐ **Another Great Day! Sunshine, if not today, maybe tomorrow. "I Love Me"**

Driving

Every person driving on the road today has learned to drive from someone's teaching, but every driver evolved to drive in a way that's more suitable to them.

through life

What works for one person doesn't work for all, and what works today may not work tomorrow.

while being mindful

If there's a family history of diabetes, high blood pressure, high cholesterol, or any other disease shortening lives and connected to food you eat; please attempt to change your family history going forward. Generational wealth in knowledge gathering, researching, and verification should also be a legacy to pass-on. Changes doesn't require immediate stop "cold turkey" or exclusion totally but modifications and moderation.

What's a work-in-progress for many of us?

Prioritize our purpose to living versus our purposes for eating or overindulging.

1. Do you eat to live or live to eat?
2. Do you eat because you're hungry or because it's timed or scheduled.
3. Is your sugar craving an added plus in your life or a sugar addiction established as a child and controlling your life?

Checkout:

To Find a Cancer Type:
https://www.cancer.gov/
https://www.cancer.org/

Diabetes:
https://www.nutrition.gov/topics/diet-and-health-conditions/diabetes
https://diabetes.org/
https://www.womenshealth.gov/cancer/breast-cancer

Heart: High Blood Pressure:
https://www.heart.org
https://www.nhlbi.nih.gov/health/high-blood-pressure

Health Disparities:
https://www.minorityhealth.hhs.gov/
https://www.healthline.com/health/racial-bias-in-healthcare
https://medlineplus.gov/blackandafricanamericanhealth.html
https://www.cdc.gov/healthequity/features/maternal-mortality/index.html

Driving through life, while being mindful that

Woke-up _____ on _____/_____/_____   M T W T F S S   Hours of sleep _____

Sunny__ Cloudy__ Rainy__ Stormy__   Lightning__ Windy__ WTHail__ Snow__ WTMother Nature__

TODAY, I AM

☐	☐	☐	☐	☐	☐	🛑	☐	☐	☐	☐	☐	☐
GREAT	HOPEFUL	AWESOME	MINDFUL	BOLD	ENCOURAGED	STOP	GROUCHY	HURT	ANGRY	MAD	BELLIGERENT	ENRAGED
GOOD	HAPPY	ACTIVE	MOTIVATED	BRILLIANT	ENERGIZED		GUARDED	HATEFUL	ANNOYED	MOODY	BITTER	EXHAUSTED

TODAY, I AM GRATEFUL & EXCITED ABOUT:

_____

_____

_____

_____

_____

_____

_____

_____

_____

_____

_____

_____

_____

_____

_____

_____

_____

_____

_____

_____

_____

_____

_____

LAST WORD IN ("Best Moment of Today" – "My Final Thought on Today" – "NOPE!, Never Again"):

$h!+ happeneds

☐ **Another Great Day! I do need others. I do need me. "I Love Me"**

Driving

The technological advancements in today's vehicles allow you to have immediate diagnostic access to your vehicle before, during, and after operations. Still, it's the in-person maintenance shop visits that diagnosis confirm and repair when attention is required.

through life

Social media platforms on numerous smart devices allow you immediate access to contacts anywhere in the world. Still, in-person contact is required to confirm whom you text, agree, disagree with, befriend, love and plan to be vulnerable with is real.

while being mindful

No one person's realness is your reality.

When visiting or interacting with family and friends, try to put visual on each other to visualize anything out of the ordinary before it increases, decreases, worsen, or something become a routine or an addiction. "How are you doing?" is a great question but your answer to "How are they looking" is a better one. Let your visual facilitate, strengthen, or refute their response.

Today's Mindful Exercise

Before your next "How are you doing?" greeting or interaction; create an open-ended response to that makes the greeter inquisitive, respond again, or be of assistance.

Open response example:

Better than yesterday!

Better than a week ago.

Better than you or better than _____ (if acquaintance).

Better than a year ago.

Better tomorrow!

Better in ___ days,

Much better than I was an hour or ____ weeks ago.

Outstanding and great today!

Awesome today!

I am so looking forward to today or tomorrow.

I need this day to be over quickly.

I am not doing so good.

I need help.

Good, I guess.

Closed example:

Okay. I'm here. Doing. I can't call it. Another day another dollar and 15 cents. Alright. Good.

Woke-up _____ on ____/____/____   M T W T F S S   Hours of sleep ____

Sunny__ Cloudy__ Rainy__ Stormy__ Lightning__ Windy__ WTHail__ Snow__ WTMother Nature__

TODAY, I AM

☐	☐	☐	☐	☐	☐	STOP	☐	☐	☐	☐	☐	☐
GREAT	HOPEFUL	AWESOME	MINDFUL	BOLD	ENCOURAGED		GROUCHY	HURT	ANGRY	MAD	BELLIGERENT	ENRAGED
GOOD	HAPPY	ACTIVE	MOTIVATED	BRILLIANT	ENERGIZED		GUARDED	HATEFUL	ANNOYED	MOODY	BITTER	EXHAUSTED

TODAY, I AM GRATEFUL & EXCITED ABOUT:

_____

_____
_____
_____
_____
_____
_____
_____
_____
_____
_____
_____
_____
_____
_____
_____
_____
_____
_____
_____
_____
_____
_____
_____
_____

LAST WORD IN ("Best Moment of Today" – "My Final Thought on Today" – "NOPE!, Never Again"):

$h!+ happeneds

☐ **Another Great Day! I'm an all-true kind human. "I Love Me"**

Driving

Try to remain calm if you're pulled over for a traffic violation. Be patient and await your time to defend in court.

through life

Try to remain calm whenever someone questions a choice you made. Be patient and await your time and action to prove them wrong.

while being mindful

In due time it's possible:

100 errors but final product for sharing or commerce at product #_____

Site or Video after #_____ search result.

Love after #_____ undesirable, "never again, my bad, or what was I thinking?"

Peace of mind after dealing with #_____ of co-workers, supervisors, or bosses.

Right or Truth after #_____ Wrongs or Lies.

Productive person and citizens after #_____ years of wrong, confinement, or hate.

Antidote or cure after specimen #_____ .

Final job offer after #_____ resumes, interviews, and tentative offers.

Final percentage after #_____ medical records, appointments, or appeals

Memorable trial defense after viewing #   case studies.

Championship after losing #_____ players, games, or seasons.

Sobriety after #_____ days of re-lapse, intervention, or rehabs

Proof and facts discovered after #_____ days in the historical trenches.

Chart topping song or movie after #_____ casting calls, talent shows, practices, auditions, venues, "no", or "Keep your day job".

Evidence with conviction after investigating and question #_____ witnesses.

What's something that took numerous times to accomplish or current number trying:

1. _____ .

2. _____ .

3. _____ .

4. _____ .

5. _____ .

Driving through life, while being mindful that

FT.GHAMBE

Woke-up _____ on _____/_____/_____   M T W T F S S   Hours of sleep _____

Sunny__ Cloudy__ Rainy__ Stormy__ Lightning__ Windy__ WTHail__ Snow__ WTMother Nature__

TODAY, I AM

☐	☐	☐	☐	☐	☐	STOP	☐	☐	☐	☐	☐	☐
GREAT	HOPEFUL	AWESOME	MINDFUL	BOLD	ENCOURAGED		GROUCHY	HURT	ANGRY	MAD	BELLIGERENT	ENRAGED
GOOD	HAPPY	ACTIVE	MOTIVATED	BRILLIANT	ENERGIZED		GUARDED	HATEFUL	ANNOYED	MOODY	BITTER	EXHAUSTED

TODAY, I AM GRATEFUL & EXCITED ABOUT:

_____

_____

_____

_____

_____

_____

_____

_____

_____

_____

_____

_____

_____

_____

_____

_____

_____

_____

_____

_____

_____

_____

_____

LAST WORD IN ("Best Moment of Today" – "My Final Thought on Today" – "NOPE!, Never Again"):

$h!+ happeneds

☐ **Another Great Day! Put my heart & mind where my eyes could see. "I Love Me"**

Driving

There will always be two sides to the story of videos capturing a law enforcer's or citizen's action that results in harm or death. Never expect the video proof captured to be the deciding factor in someone's guilt or innocence.

through life

There are always two sides to the story. Never assume the truth to be believed because some individual's assumptions have been known to morph a lie into truth.

while being mindful

There are always two-sided to the story:

1. Police vs. Public
2. Harasser vs. Harassed
3. Abuser vs. Abused
4. Truth vs. Lies
5. Bully vs. Bullied
6. Victim's side vs. Subject's side
7. Vehicle occupant's side vs. Eyewitness's side
8. Morally vs. Immorally
9. Past exclusive CRT structured vs. Current inclusive CRT outrages
10. Slaves vs. Slave and Plantation owners
11. Prosecutor's side (guilty) vs. Defendant's lawyer side (not guilty)
12. Liked vs. Love
13. Florida's education vs Florida's education
14. Scammer vs. Scammed
15. Democrat vs. Republican
16. Past vs. Today
17. Social media posts vs. Not usually part of my character.
18. Has a crush vs. Creepy
19. Superfan vs. Stalker
20. Political campaign vs Elected official
21. **Left vs. Right** (Political Left & Right explained as from the Military's Left & Right point of view):
    a) It's true, for the majority; everybody was home when you left. *Family's Political Party views, association, and views.*
    b) You have to face left or right face or go about face (which doesn't move you forward) until *Forward-March.*
    c) You can start off stepping to the left or to the right but not forever. *Left Step-March*
    d) You have to look to your left and right to be properly on line.
    e) When firing on the qual range, you must scan to your left and right for correct target engagement. *To receive a "Go" at the station.*
    *Just make sure you're on the side of right- Human Right

Woke-up _____ on ____/_____/_____   M T W T F S S   Hours of sleep ____

Sunny__ Cloudy__ Rainy__ Stormy__ Lightning__ Windy__ WTHail__ Snow__ WTMother Nature__

TODAY, I AM

☐	☐	☐	☐	☐	☐	STOP	☐	☐	☐	☐	☐	☐
GREAT	HOPEFUL	AWESOME	MINDFUL	BOLD	ENCOURAGED		GROUCHY	HURT	ANGRY	MAD	BELLIGERENT	ENRAGED
GOOD	HAPPY	ACTIVE	MOTIVATED	BRILLIANT	ENERGIZED		GUARDED	HATEFUL	ANNOYED	MOODY	BITTER	EXHAUSTED

TODAY, I AM GRATEFUL & EXCITED ABOUT:

_____

_____

_____

_____

_____

_____

_____

_____

_____

_____

_____

_____

_____

_____

_____

_____

_____

_____

_____

_____

_____

_____

_____

_____

_____

LAST WORD IN ("Best Moment of Today" – "My Final Thought on Today" – "NOPE!, Never Again"):

$h!+ happeneds

☐ **Another Great Day! Me, Myself, and I. "I Love Me"**

Driving

What do you think about my driving? Anyone that asks the question already knows their answer.

through life

You will be asked questions with the answer already known:

- A parent's way to test your honesty and maturity.
- A spouse way to test your vows and trustworthiness.
- A cop way to test your involvement, guilt, and legal knowledge.
- A lawyer's way to test your testimony.
- A friend's way to test your loyalty.
- A leader or supervisor's way to test your integrity.
- A spirited person's way to test your faith.
- An internet predator's way to test your maturity, loneliness, and availability.
- An internet love connection way to test your desperateness, loneliness, and finances.
- A dental and medical facilities way to test if you're destitute or insured and covered.
- An employer way to test your aptitude for a job.
- A con artists way to test your ignorance.
- A devil-spirited person's way to test your faith.
- A bigot's way to test tolerance or bigotry.
- A family member's way to test your giving, regrets, or kindness.
- A car salesperson's way to test if you know your credit score.
- An internal test of your own integrity, loyalty, faith, judgement, or morality.

while being mindful

Bypass individuals who show they're incapable of change for the greater you. People don't mean to F*>K you, but they'll F*>K" you every time if it's a choice between you or their family, freedom, dignity, or livelihood.

0001 ANOTHER ONE!

Woke-up _____ on ____/____/____ M T W T F S S Hours of sleep ____

Sunny__ Cloudy__ Rainy__ Stormy__ Lightning__ Windy__ WTHail__ Snow__ WTMother Nature__

TODAY, I AM

☐ ☐ ☐ ☐ ☐ ☐ STOP ☐ ☐ ☐ ☐ ☐ ☐

| GREAT | HOPEFUL | AWESOME | MINDFUL | BOLD | ENCOURAGED | | GROUCHY | HURT | ANGRY | MAD | BELLIGERENT | ENRAGED |
| GOOD | HAPPY | ACTIVE | MOTIVATED | BRILLIANT | ENERGIZED | | GUARDED | HATEFUL | ANNOYED | MOODY | BITTER | EXHAUSTED |

TODAY, I AM GRATEFUL & EXCITED ABOUT:

_____

_____
_____
_____
_____
_____
_____
_____
_____
_____
_____
_____
_____
_____
_____
_____
_____
_____
_____
_____
_____
_____
_____

LAST WORD IN ("Best Moment of Today" – "My Final Thought on Today" – "NOPE!, Never Again"):

$h!+ happeneds

☐ **Approved. Another Great Day! "I Love Me"**

Driving

You are driving through a parking lot and see a vehicle with its reverse lights on backing into your traffic flow. What should you do?

1. Stop and allow?
2. Alert? (Blow horn/flashlight/yell)
3. Proceed and hope they see you but with your foot & hand hovering over the brakes & horn?
4. Proceed while fuming? (I wish they would!)

through life

You witness someone about to do something wrong, spiteful, immoral, hateful, racist, anti-national, or discriminative. What should you do?

1. Stop and observe?
2. Record for viral wickedness?
3. Alert them ("I see you") and Alert others ("Do you see what I see?")
4. Report?
5. Post on social media?
6. Approach with caution & give "better choices" wisdom/option?
7. Mind your business?

while being mindful

Do not be afraid to be different or try something different to help someone who may need a different approach:

- Calmness instead of mirroring same energy
- Oneness instead of stereotyping
- Compassion instead of being judgmental
- Listening instead of enforcing
- Attentiveness instead of deflecting
- Empathy instead of projecting
- Assisting and requesting other assistance instead of video recording

It takes awhile

Every person won't feel they need someone's assistance, even if it's obvious to those awaiting to assist or rescue.

Woke-up _____ on ____/_____/_____   M T W T F S S   Hours of sleep ____

Sunny__ Cloudy__ Rainy__ Stormy__ Lightning__ Windy__ WTHail__ Snow__ WTMother Nature__

TODAY, I AM

☐	☐	☐	☐	☐	☐	**STOP**	☐	☐	☐	☐	☐	☐
GREAT	HOPEFUL	AWESOME	MINDFUL	BOLD	ENCOURAGED		GROUCHY	HURT	ANGRY	MAD	BELLIGERENT	ENRAGED
GOOD	HAPPY	ACTIVE	MOTIVATED	BRILLIANT	ENERGIZED		GUARDED	HATEFUL	ANNOYED	MOODY	BITTER	EXHAUSTED

TODAY, I AM GRATEFUL & EXCITED ABOUT:

_____

_____

_____

_____

_____

LAST WORD IN ("Best Moment of Today" – "My Final Thought on Today" – "NOPE!, Never Again"):

$h!+ happeneds

☐ **My motto or mantra: Another Great Day! "I Love Me"**

Driving

What do you do if you witness a traffic accident? Help or Get Help!

through life

What do you do if you witness someone causing harm to oneself or another? Help or Get Help!

while being mindful

How can you help?

- Help Self: Make sure you are safe and not in danger first.
- Call for Help- 911
- Yell for Help – for witness/assistance
- Provide Help – give aid, comfort, and refuge
- Wait for Help - emergency service professionals' arrival
- Help more- don't touch or move anything if possible but observe, video, or take a photo to document and recall when needed.

Help but never lose focus of "You and Yours":

Driving: What can happen if you're too inquisitive of an accident scene aftermath or tow vehicle clean-up of wrecked vehicles while driving past? Are you more likely to lose focus and rear-end vehicle ahead.

Relationship: What can happen if your too inquisitive or too involved in someone else's relationship or life more than yours? Are you more likely to lose yourself, your relationship, and possibly hinder the next.

Woke-up _____ on ____/____/____ M T W T F S S Hours of sleep ____

Sunny_ Cloudy_ Rainy_ Stormy_ Lightning_ Windy_ WTHail_ Snow_ WTMother Nature_

TODAY, I AM

☐	☐	☐	☐	☐	☐	STOP	☐	☐	☐	☐	☐	☐
GREAT	HOPEFUL	AWESOME	MINDFUL	BOLD	ENCOURAGED		GROUCHY	HURT	ANGRY	MAD	BELLIGERENT	ENRAGED
GOOD	HAPPY	ACTIVE	MOTIVATED	BRILLIANT	ENERGIZED		GUARDED	HATEFUL	ANNOYED	MOODY	BITTER	EXHAUSTED

TODAY, I AM GRATEFUL & EXCITED ABOUT:

_____

_____

_____

_____

_____

LAST WORD IN ("Best Moment of Today" – "My Final Thought on Today" – "NOPE!, Never Again"):

$h!+ happeneds

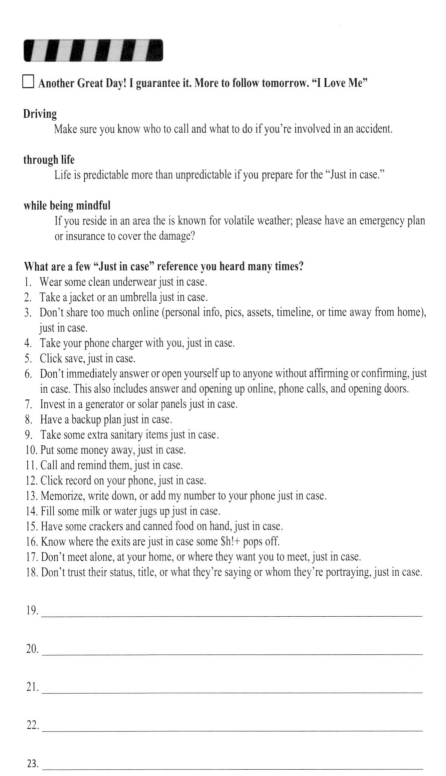

☐ **Another Great Day! I guarantee it. More to follow tomorrow. "I Love Me"**

Driving
Make sure you know who to call and what to do if you're involved in an accident.

through life
Life is predictable more than unpredictable if you prepare for the "Just in case."

while being mindful
If you reside in an area the is known for volatile weather; please have an emergency plan or insurance to cover the damage?

What are a few "Just in case" reference you heard many times?
1. Wear some clean underwear just in case.
2. Take a jacket or an umbrella just in case.
3. Don't share too much online (personal info, pics, assets, timeline, or time away from home), just in case.
4. Take your phone charger with you, just in case.
5. Click save, just in case.
6. Don't immediately answer or open yourself up to anyone without affirming or confirming, just in case. This also includes answer and opening up online, phone calls, and opening doors.
7. Invest in a generator or solar panels just in case.
8. Have a backup plan just in case.
9. Take some extra sanitary items just in case.
10. Put some money away, just in case.
11. Call and remind them, just in case.
12. Click record on your phone, just in case.
13. Memorize, write down, or add my number to your phone just in case.
14. Fill some milk or water jugs up just in case.
15. Have some crackers and canned food on hand, just in case.
16. Know where the exits are just in case some $h!+ pops off.
17. Don't meet alone, at your home, or where they want you to meet, just in case.
18. Don't trust their status, title, or what they're saying or whom they're portraying, just in case.

19. _____

20. _____

21. _____

22. _____

23. _____

Driving through life, while being mindful that

0001 ANOTHER ONE!

Woke-up _____ on _____/_____/_____   M T W T F S S   Hours of sleep _____

Sunny__ Cloudy__ Rainy__ Stormy__ Lightning__ Windy__ WTHail__ Snow__ WTMother Nature__

TODAY, I AM

☐	☐	☐	☐	☐	☐	STOP	☐	☐	☐	☐	☐	☐
GREAT	HOPEFUL	AWESOME	MINDFUL	BOLD	ENCOURAGED		GROUCHY	HURT	ANGRY	MAD	BELLIGERENT	ENRAGED
GOOD	HAPPY	ACTIVE	MOTIVATED	BRILLIANT	ENERGIZED		GUARDED	HATEFUL	ANNOYED	MOODY	BITTER	EXHAUSTED

TODAY, I AM GRATEFUL & EXCITED ABOUT:

_____

_____

_____

_____

_____

_____

_____

_____

_____

_____

_____

_____

_____

_____

_____

_____

_____

_____

_____

_____

_____

_____

_____

_____

_____

_____

LAST WORD IN ("Best Moment of Today" – "My Final Thought on Today" – "NOPE!, Never Again"):

$h!+ happeneds

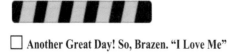

☐ **Another Great Day! So, Brazen. "I Love Me"**

Driving

Don't put your vehicle on display in an auto show if you don't want others staring, taking pictures, sharing, and judging.

through life

Don't put your body or life on internet display if you don't want others staring, sharing, capturing, and judging. If you do, please prepare for yourself for the trolls and those individuals who love to stir and illuminate other mess than deal with personal mess.

while being mindful

How would you know if a photo or video you shared for one isn't being shared with another person, a group of people, and so on?

- The quality and digitalization of photos have improved and changed to where you'll fade in real life before the digital photo fades. A careless embarrassing photo you share with someone you no longer date, love, or are familiar with is the same clear picture that will be available to the college you applied to, future employers, co-workers, new friends, social groups, spouses, in-laws, political voters, and children and their children's children.

- Most relationships don't evolve to happiness ever after. Suppose you know of many first relationships (high school, college, military initial training, or moment of temptations and convenience) ending badly.

- If you are aware of sextortion happening after others exchange personal pictures online with someone, they hoped was genuine, truthful, or a friend. Why would you so nonchalantly engage and exchange compromising and embarrassing texts, photos, or videos? Do you know the close friends of the individual whom they may share your personal shares? With technology today, do you know whom you're trusting and sharing your vulnerability with. What do you have to lose if the person(s) you share, shares without your consent or blackmails you once, twice, or until you're can't sustain the next request?

- Lastly, don't be so quick to give away your personal goodness (mental or physical) online to the hacks and hackers? Meaning: Do you know the security safeguards and protections measure of the individual you're sharing in private with? Do you know the security software of the other person's devices? Do you know who else has access to their device? Be your only fan until you're ready to share on your own accord.

- What is Sexploitation? Do your research on Sexploitation Scams. Do a quick search of the news about sextortion cases. Make sure the teens in your family or bubble are aware of one of many online dangers. Young males are the most exploited.

Sharing too much of yourself way too soon

Should any of the above knowledge make you more apprehensive in sharing risky pictures and videos online or uncommitted relationship? What will happen to those intimate and personal shared embarrassing or scandalous communications upon the relationship's breakup? First time madly in love partners, please know the answer before you show.

Driving through life, while being mindful that

Woke-up _____ on ____/_____/_____   M T W T F S S   Hours of sleep ____

Sunny__ Cloudy__ Rainy__ Stormy__ Lightning__ Windy__ WTHail__ Snow__ WTMother Nature__

TODAY, I AM

☐	☐	☐	☐	☐	☐	STOP	☐	☐	☐	☐	☐	☐
GREAT	HOPEFUL	AWESOME	MINDFUL	BOLD	ENCOURAGED		GROUCHY	HURT	ANGRY	MAD	BELLIGERENT	ENRAGED
GOOD	HAPPY	ACTIVE	MOTIVATED	BRILLIANT	ENERGIZED		GUARDED	HATEFUL	ANNOYED	MOODY	BITTER	EXHAUSTED

TODAY, I AM GRATEFUL & EXCITED ABOUT:

_____

_____

_____

_____

_____

_____

_____

_____

_____

_____

_____

_____

_____

_____

_____

_____

_____

_____

_____

_____

_____

_____

_____

LAST WORD IN ("Best Moment of Today" – "My Final Thought on Today" – "NOPE!, Never Again"):

$h!+ happeneds

Hello: *"I'm blank page, I was left here on purpose"*

As the Author Defines

Ass As is or the Ass in you or someone.

Black Black loving and celebrating kinship (w/*caution*: All kinfolks ain't your folks)
Blacks Black loving all created kindred spirits
BLaKBlack Black Limiting and Killing Black. Black on black crime/killing, jonesing jealousy,
or BLaKBrown self-hate, and committing black genocide within as planned, structured,
implemented, and manipulated by the WHAAATE People's WHAAATE Loss Plan.
The plan implemented to minimize, shed, surgically remove, or erase blackness.

Finacial Financial prejudice and bigotry toward a person based on their race only.

NON-Whites No Objective Nonsense-We help inclusivity to elevate society

OKAYE Own Kind Against Your Existent

RHACISTS Ratchet Humans Advancing Cultured Institutionalized Superiority Taught $h!+

SHH! Solidarity, Hope, and Happiness!

$h!+ **"Sugar honey iced tea"** 1. Oldest School: "Societies' hate is taught" (taught to
empower, manipulate, finance, and divide, while being disguised through many
individuals' interpretations and teachings).
2. Symbolizes: "Money, Humanism, Strong Emotions, and other Added Stuff"

$h!+ happened **Past "Sugar honey iced tea"** 1. an experience. 2. a part of your past

$h!+ happen **Present "Sugar honey iced tea"** 1. Just occurred. 2. We're still paying high
interest rate daily on being an American citizen because of groups and
organization's Financial Interest, Special Interest, Corporate Interest, Political
Interest, Lobbyist Interest, Religious Interest, Racial and Power Interest being
raised as your reading this.

$h!+ happens **Ongoing "Sugar honey iced tea" (same $h!+ different generation, politicians,
greed, and power grabbers) Ex.** 1. 3% vs Rich vs. Middle Class vs. Poor vs.
Below Poverty 2. Race vs. Race 3. Republican vs Democrats 4. Fearmongering
Tactics vs Saviors Tactics. 5. Religion vs Religions. 6. Laws being changed or
interpreted to divide the bottom, confuse the middle, and sustain the top 7.
Gerrymandering 8. Voting rights 9. Citizen rights 10. Protests 11. Competition

Same but Tomato-Tomato, Potato-Potato Democrat-Republican
pronounced Religion- My/Our Interpretation Data-Data
differently Laws-Empowered Interpretation Phuket (English)-Phuket (Thai)
Martinez-Martinez, Georgia Rights-Our Rights- Our Group's Rights
Haaate-Racist-Racism-Bigots Profit schemes/non-profiting schemes
New Orleans-New Orleans I lost the election-Voting System broken
Long-Time Friend-Lobbyist-Donor My Rights/Choice-My Right to Vote out
Curriculum-System-Funded Human-Races-Citizen- "We the People"

Driving through life, while being mindful that $h!+ happeneds

WHAAATE	**WHAAATE PEOPLE:** Individual Willfully Hating Anyone Advancing Anything Toward Equality (HAAATE that includes hating whites (defined below), and others categorized as non-whites. Additionally, there are **IHAAATE PEOPLE (two type):** Individuals Historically Against Advancing Anything Toward Equality Instigators Hating Anyone Advancing Anything Toward Equality
White	Individual Willfully helping inclusivity toward equality
Whites	Individuals Willfully helping inclusivity to equalize society

WTH   **"Writing Tomorrow's History"**

"What The Hell"

"Way Too Harsh"

"Why The Hate?"

"Where's The Hope?"

"Why The Hush?"

"Why The Hipocracy/Hysteria/Hesitation?" 🙁 **WTH?**

<u>Who are you tomorrow</u>?

Will you be:

Black or BlakBlack/Brown?

WHAAATE or White?

RHACIST or Righteous?

OKAYE or Okay with every human being?

IHAAATE PEOPLE or "WE THE PEOPLE"

Driving through life, while being mindful that $h!+ happeneds

"Writing Tomorrow's History"

Made in the USA
Columbia, SC
03 March 2024

32249880R00113